5|18

lone

D0439960

Pocket
FLORENCE & TUSCANY

TOP SIGHTS • LOCAL LIFE • MADE EASY

Nicola Williams
Virginia Maxwell

In This Book

QuickStart Guide

Your keys to understanding the region – we help you decide what to do and how to do it

Need to Know
Tips for a smooth trip

Neighbourhoods
What's where

Explore Florence & Tuscany

The best things to see and do, neighbourhood by neighbourhood

Top Sights
Make the most of your visit

Local Life
The insider's region

The Best of Florence & Tuscany

The highlights in handy lists to help you plan

Best Walks
See the city on foot

Florence & Tuscany's Best...
The best experiences

Survival Guide

Tips and tricks for a seamless, hassle-free experience

Getting Around
Travel like a local

Essential Information
Including where to stay

Our selection of the region's best places to eat, drink and experience:

⊙ **Sights**

⊗ **Eating**

⊖ **Drinking**

✪ **Entertainment**

🔒 **Shopping**

These symbols give you the vital information for each listing:

☏ Telephone Numbers
🕓 Opening Hours
P Parking
🚭 Nonsmoking
@ Internet Access
📶 Wi-Fi Access
🥗 Vegetarian Selection
📖 English-Language Menu

👪 Family-Friendly
🐾 Pet-Friendly
🚌 Bus
⛴ Ferry
M Metro
S Subway
🚊 Tram
🚆 Train

Find each listing quickly on maps for each neighbourhood:

Bar Hemingway

16 ⊖ Map p233, B2

Legend has it that Hemi
self, wielding a machine
erate this timber-pan
ered bar during
showpiece is a
n by Papa ar
town. Dress
s.com; Hôtel Rit ⊙6.30pm-2a

Lonely Planet's Florence & Tuscany

Lonely Planet Pocket Guides are designed to get you straight to the heart of the city.

Inside you'll find all the must-see sights, plus tips to make your visit to each one really memorable. We've split the city into easy-to-navigate neighbourhoods and provided clear maps so you'll find your way around with ease. Our expert authors have searched out the best of the city: walks, food, nightlife and shopping, to name a few. Because you want to explore, our 'Local Life' pages will take you to some of the most exciting areas to experience the real Florence & Tuscany.

And of course you'll find all the practical tips you need for a smooth trip: itineraries for short visits, how to get around, and how much to tip the guy who serves you a drink at the end of a long day's exploration.

It's your guarantee of a really great experience.

Our Promise

You can trust our travel information because Lonely Planet authors visit the places we write about, each and every edition. We never accept freebies for positive coverage, so you can rely on us to tell it like it is.

QuickStart Guide 7

Explore Florence & Tuscany 21

Worth a Trip:

The Best of Florence & Tuscany 157

Florence & Tuscany's Best Walks

Florence & Tuscany's Best ...

Survival Guide 177

QuickStart Guide

Welcome to Florence & Tuscany

Though surprisingly small, Florence (Firenze) is laden with cultural attractions and charm. Medieval streets evoke a thousand tales, and museums and churches safeguard the world's greatest repository of Renaissance art. Nearby destinations, including Siena, Pisa, Chianti, San Gimignano and Lucca, are similarly alluring, and are easily visited on day trips.

Duomo (p24)
AB_ICP/ALAMY STOCK PHOTO ©

Florence & Tuscany
Top Sights

Duomo (p24)

Florence's iconic landmark.

Galleria degli Uffizi (p30)

Europe's finest Renaissance art collection.

Galleria dell'Accademia (p64)

The world's most famous statue.

Basilica di Santa Maria Novella (p50)

Renaissance magnificence in a sacred monastery.

Palazzo Pitti (p100)

Museum meanderings in a Renaissance palace.

Basilica di Santa Croce (p84)

Frescoed chapels and famous graves.

Museo del Bargello (p86)

Italy's finest collection of Tuscan Renaissance sculpture.

Opera della Metropolitana di Siena (p140)

Arranged around Siena's *duomo* is a cluster of ecclesiastical buildings.

Piazza dei Miracoli, Pisa (p128)

Pisa's 'Field of Miracles' is one of Italy's major tourist drawcards.

Lucca (p136)

Lovely Lucca endears itself to everyone who visits.

San Gimignano (p154)

A walled hilltop town that lures summer day-trippers.

Chianti (p152)

A postcard-perfect part of Tuscany.

Florence & Tuscany Local Life

Local experiences and hidden gems to help you uncover the real region

Florence's 377,000 residents enjoy a lifestyle that is crammed with culture, back-dropped by history and anchored by family, faith and food. Head to their neighbourhoods, churches, cafes and restaurants to see what makes life here so special.

A Boutique Shopping Spree (p34)

☑ Historical cafes ☑ Fashion and art boutiques

A Day in Fiesole (p80)

☑ Romantic city views ☑ Historic buildings

A Night Out in Santa Croce (p88)

☑ Bars and clubs ☑ Fabulous dining

Other great places to experience the region like a local:

Le Passeggiata (p40)

Cocktail Culture (p124)

Wine tasting (p123)

Tripe Carts (p42)

Third-Wave Coffee & Gin (p96)

Riverside Street Food (p95)

Lunch at the Market (p92)

A Secret Garden (p120)

Picnic Perfect (p59)

Hipster Hang-out (p73)

City of Artisans (p114)

☑ Artisan workshops ☑ Independent designer boutiques

Florence & Tuscany
Day Planner

Day One

☀ Journey into the Renaissance with a morning of mind-blowing 15th- and 16th-century art at the **Galleria degli Uffizi** (p30). Break for coffee on the rooftop terrace where the Medici clan would listen to music on the square below. Post-museum, clear your head with a **Piazza della Signoria** (p39) stroll.

☀ Meander south to the river and cross **Ponte Vecchio** (p122). Look for hacked street signs by **Clet** (p110) in this bohemian neck of the woods – buy postcards to send home at his art studio here. Explore **Basilica di Santo Spirito** (p118) and magnificent **Cappella Brancacci** (p118; reservation required), grabbing a quick coffee or tea at the Oltrarno branch of **Ditta Artigianale** (p124). As the sun sinks, hike uphill to **Piazzale Michelangelo** (p106) for swoon-worthy views of the city followed by *aperitivi* (pre-dinner drinks) at **Le Volpi e l'Uva** (p109).

☾ Stay on the Oltrarno for a sensational dinner at **Essenziale** (p119) or **Burro e Acciughe** (p120). Afterwards, hit the on-trend, bar-busy district of San Frediano for craft cocktails at **Mad Souls & Spirits** (p123) or **Dolce Vita** (p125). Later, track down **Rasputin** (p123), the city's secret speakeasy open until the wee hours.

Day Two

☀ Prepare yourself for monumental sacred art and architecture on Piazza del Duomo: visit the **cathedral** (p24), climb up its **campanile** (p26), duck into its **baptistry** (p26) and end on a giddy high with a hike up into the frescoed dome of Brunelleschi's **cupola** (p25). Complete the story inside the **Grande Museo del Duomo** (p27).

☀ Lunch at **Irene** (p40) or **Trattoria Le Mossacce** (p41). Window-shop on Via de' Tornabuoni, breaking for a cheeky truffle *panino* (sandwich) at **Procacci** (p46) or drink at fashionable **Caffè Giacosa** (p57). Mooch west, along boutique shopping streets Via della Spada or Via della Vigna Nova, to **Basilica di Santa Maria Novella** (p50). If you have time, modern-art museum **Museo Novecento** (p54) is superb. Cross Ponte alla Carraia and savour a gourmet *aperitivo* at **Il Santino** (p123) or Japanese-inspired sake cocktails at **Kawaii** (p124).

☾ Dine by candlelight at **Il Santo Bevitore** (p119). For *dolci* (sweets) grab a gelato from **Gelateria La Carraia** (p122) to enjoy over a scenic riverside walk by night. Later, dance to spaghetti jazz and quaff cocktails beneath the stars at **Santarosa Bistrot** (p122).

Short on time?

We've arranged Florence & Tuscany's must-sees into these day-by-day itineraries to make sure you see the very best of the region in the time you have available.

Day Three

☀ Begin the day in San Marco with a glorious 360-degree admiration of the world's most famous naked man, Michelangelo's original *David*, at the **Galleria dell'Accademia** (p64). Continue to the soulfully uplifting **Museo di San Marco** (p69), followed by a cappuccino or specialist coffee at **Ditta Al Cinema** (p74). End the morning with the emotive **Museo degli Innocenti** (p70).

☀ Grab a quick lunch at **Pugi** (p74) or lounge with hipsters at **La Ménagère** (p71). Saunter south to Piazza della Signoria where the city's most famous David copy guards Palazzo Vecchio. Duck east to **Museo del Bargello** (p86) to admire David versions by Donatello and Andrea Verrocchio, then nip back to **Palazzo Vecchio** (p38) in time to visit the fortress palace and catch sunset views from the top of its striking Torre d'Arnolfo – a Florentine landmark. Savour a hot chocolate at **Caffè Rivoire** (p34) or an *aperitivo* at **Coquinarius** (p44).

☾ Dine at **Il Teatro del Sale** (p89) or **Trattoria Cibrèo** (p92). If the former, sit back and enjoy the theatre show. Otherwise, explore the happening district of Santa Croce by night.

Day Four

☀ Begin with a gulp of coffee and daily Florentine life inside San Lorenzo's buzzing **Mercato Centrale** (p71) then weave your way south to your next ports of call: **Basilica di San Lorenzo** (p68), **Biblioteca Medicea Laurenziana** (p68) and absolutely dazzling **Museo delle Cappelle Medicee** (p68), a must-see for Michelangelo lovers. End with a market eatery lunch: at **Da Nerbone** (p72), **Trattoria Mario** (p71) or the **Mercato Centrale** (p71) food hall on the first floor.

☀ Spend the afternoon exploring the galleries and garden of the monumental **Palazzo Pitti** (p100), home at various times to members of the powerful Medici, Lorraine and Savoy families. Be sure to pop into the nearby **Giardino Bardini** (p106) – a path links it with Pitti's Giardino di Boboli – and end with an early-evening drink across from the palace at **Enoteca Pitti Gola e Cantina** (p123).

☾ Dinner is an upmarket affair, highly memorable, at **La Leggenda dei Frati** (p107) or **San Niccolò 39** (p108). After dinner, hobnob with hipster Florentines over a cocktail nightcap and twinkling night-time views up high at **Flò** (p109).

Need to Know

For more information,
see Survival Guide (p177)

Currency
Euro (€)

Language
Italian

Visas
Not needed for residents of Schengen
countries or for many visitors staying for
less than 90 days.

Money
ATMs widely available. Credit cards
accepted at most hotels and many
restaurants.

Mobile Phones
Local SIM cards can be used in European
and Australian phones. Other phones must
be set to roaming.

Time
Italy operates on a 24-hour clock. It is one
hour ahead of GMT/UTC. Daylight-saving
time starts on the last Sunday in March,
when clocks are put forward one hour. Clocks
are put back an hour on the last Sunday in
October.

Tipping
Locals don't generally tip waiters, but most
visitors leave 10% to 15% in restaurants if
there's no service charge. Round taxi fares up
to the nearest euro.

① Before You Go

Your Daily Budget

Budget: Less than €90
▶ Dorm bed: €18–45
▶ Sandwich: €3–8
▶ Trattoria dinner: €15–25

Midrange: €90–200
▶ Double room in a midrange hotel:
€110–200
▶ Restaurant meal: €30–45
▶ Aperitivo: €10

Top End: More than €200
▶ Double room in a four- or five-star hotel:
€200 plus
▶ Upmarket restaurant meal: €45–70
▶ Walking tours: €20–50

Useful Websites

Lonely Planet (www.lonelyplanet.com/italy/
florence) Destination information.

The Florentine (www.theflorentine.net)
English-language newspaper.

Girl in Florence (www.girlinflorence.com)
Smart drinking 'n dining recommenda-
tions from American Georgette, at home in
Florence.

Lost in Florence (www.lostinflorence.it)
Boutique openings in the city.

Advance Planning

Three months before Buy tickets for
springtime's Maggio Musicale Fiorentino.

One month before Book tickets online
for the Uffizi, Galleria dell'Accademia and
Brunelleschi's cupola at the Duomo.

One week before Make table reservations
at gastronomic hot spots Essenziale and
La Leggenda dei Frati.

2 Arriving in Florence & Tuscany

Most people arrive one of two ways: by air to international airports in **Florence** (Aeroporto Amerigo Vespucci; ☎055 3 06 15, 055 306 18 30; www.aeroporto.firenze.it; Via del Termine 11), 5km northwest of the city centre, or **Pisa** (Galileo Galilei Airport; ☎050 84 93 00; www.pisa-airport.com), 80km west of Florence; or by train to Stazione Campo di Marte or Stazione di Santa Maria Novella, both in central Florence.

✈ From Florence Airport

Shuttle buses to the city centre **bus station** (Autostazione Busitalia-Sita Nord; ☎800 373760; Via Santa Caterina da Siena 17r; ⏱5.30am-8.30pm Mon-Sat, 6am-8pm Sun) every 30 minutes between 6am and 8.30pm, then hourly 8.30pm to 11.30pm. Taxis are set at €20 to the city centre (€24 on Sundays and holidays, €25.30 between 10pm and 6am), plus €1 per bag and €1 supplement for fourth passenger. Exit the terminal building, bear right and you'll come to the taxi rank.

✈ From Pisa International Airport

Regular trains and buses between 4.30am and 10.25pm to Florence's main train station, Stazione di Santa Maria Novella; count on €5 to €10 and 1½ hours journey time.

🚉 Stazione di Santa Maria Novella

You are in the city centre; Piazza del Duomo is an easy 10-minute walk away.

3 Getting Around

Florence is mostly easily explored on foot, so tourists have little need to use the city's transport. Exceptions are the bus services to Fiesole and Piazzale Michelangelo.

Siena and San Gimignano are easily accessed from Florence by bus. Pisa and Lucca are best reached by train. To explore Chianti you need a car.

🚗 Car & Motorcycle

There are strict ZTLs (*Zone a Traffico Limitato;* Limited Traffic Zones) in Florence, Siena, Pisa, Lucca and San Gimignano. If you drive in them you risk a fine of up to €200. Visit www.comune.fi.it for a map of Florence's ZTL.

🚌 Bus

In Florence, buses and electric minibuses – including bus 13 to Piazzale Michelangelo – start/terminate at the ATAF bus stops opposite the southeastern exit of Stazione di Santa Maria Novella. Tickets cost €1.20 (€2 on board – drivers don't give change!) and are sold at kiosks, tobacconists and at the **ATAF ticket & information office** (☎800 424500, 199 104245; www.ataf.net; Stazione di Santa Maria Novella, Piazza della Stazione; ⏱6.45am-8pm Mon-Sat) inside the main ticketing hall at Stazione di Santa Maria Novella. A travel pass valid for one/three/ seven days is €5/12/18. Upon boarding, time stamp your ticket (punch on board) or risk an on-the-spot €50 fine.

🚗 Taxi

Taxis can't be hailed in the street. Ranks are found close to train and bus stations; in Florence call ☎055 42 42 or 055 43 90.

🚉 Train

The Italian rail network **Trenitalia** (www. trenitalia.com) is modern and efficient. Check its website for routes, timetables and fares.

Florence & Tuscany
Neighbourhoods

Worth a Trip

○ **Local Life**

A Day in Fiesole (p80)

Santa Maria Novella (p48)

Shoppers have long been drawn to this chic corner of the city, lured by the sophisticated boutiques on Via de' Tornabuoni.

👁 **Top Sights**

Basilica di Santa Maria Novella

Oltrarno (p112)

A beguiling labyrinth of cobbled streets and hidden piazzas sheltering traditional *botteghe* (artisans workshops), bohemian wine bars and foodie hotspots.

Boboli & San Miniato al Monte (p98)

A profusion of parks, gardens and panoramic terraces stretching from the Arno to Piazzale Michelangelo.

👁 **Top Sights**

Palazzo Pitti

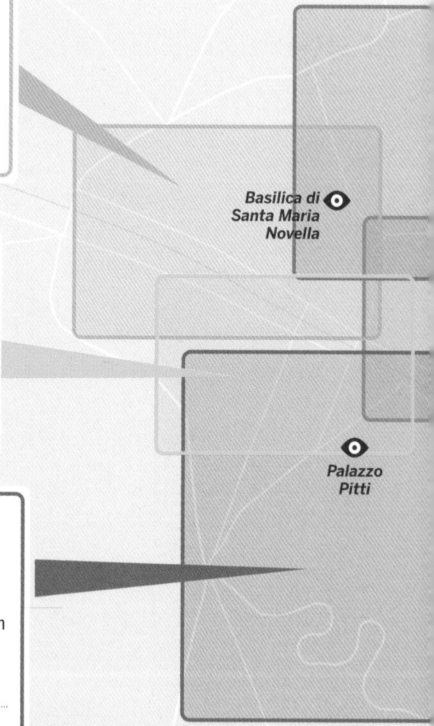

Basilica di 👁
Santa Maria
Novella

👁
Palazzo
Pitti

**San Lorenzo &
San Marco (p62)**
This is Medici territory –
home to the family's
mansion, parish church
and mausoleum.

◉ Top Sights
Galleria dell'Accademia

Worth a Trip
◉ Top Sights
Piazza dei Miracoli (Pisa)
(p128)

Lucca (p136)

Opera della Metropolitana di Siena (Siena)
(p140)

Chianti (p152)

San Gimignano (p154)

◉ *Galleria
dell'Accademia*

◉ *Duomo*

◉ *Museo del
Bargello*

◉ *Basilica di
Santa Croce*

◉
*Galleria degli
Uffizi*

**Duomo to Piazza
della Signoria
(p22)**
The world-famous
Galleria degli Uffizi is
one of many marvellous
museums found in the
city's medieval heart.

◉ Top Sights
Duomo

Galleria degli Uffizi

Santa Croce (p82)
The advent of
ultrafashionable
eateries, bars and clubs
has reinvented this
ancient residential area.

◉ Top Sights
Museo del Bargello

Basilica di Santa Croce

Explore
Florence & Tuscany

View of Florence and the Ponte Vecchio (p122) from the
Giardino di Boboli (p103)
BRIAN KINNEY/SHUTTERSTOCK ©

Explore

Duomo to Piazza della Signoria

Hub of the Renaissance and cosmopolitan heart of modern Florence, the enchanting maze of narrow streets between the Duomo and Piazza della Signoria packs one almighty historic and cultural punch. A 'hood harking back to Dante, the Romans and beyond, this is where the city's blockbuster sights – and tourists – mingle with elegant cafes, chic boutiques and the city's swishest shopping strip.

The Sights in a Day

☼ Kick-start the day on **Piazza della Repubblica** (p39) with a quick coffee at historic cafe **Gilli** (p44) or bespoke latte or protein-powered smoothie at nearby **Shake Café** (p46), then head towards the river. Pause en route to admire the exquisite sculpted facade of **Chiesa e Museo di Orsanmichele** (p39) en route. Devote the morning to world-class art at the **Galleria degli Uffizi** (pictured left; p30).

☼ Grab a quick gourmet *panini* (sandwich), washed down with a glass of Tuscan wine or craft beer, at stylish sandiwch bar, **'Ino** (p42), and afterwards, an alfresco coffee on **Piazza della Signoria** (p39). Then dive straight into **Palazzo Vecchio** (p38), not missing the bewitching view from its tower. Devote the remainder of the afternoon to the city's iconic **Duomo** (p24).

☾ Come *aperitivo* (pre-dinner drinks accompanied by cocktail snacks) hour, hit the river for a photogenic stroll along the Arno and its dusk-kissed bridges. Watch the sun set over a drink on the chic rooftop terrace of **La Terrazza Lounge Bar** (p43). Later, indulge in a delicious dinner of outstanding modern Tuscan cuisine at chic bistro **Irene** (p40).

For a local's day around the Duomo and Piazza della Signoria, see p34.

◉ Top Sights

Duomo (p24)

Galleria degli Uffizi (p30)

◯ Local Life

A Boutique Shopping Spree (p34)

♥ Best of Florence

Eating

Irene (p40)

Osteria Il Buongustai (p41)

Gelateria Pasticceria Badiani (p44)

Trattoria Le Mossacce (p41)

'Ino (p42)

Drinking

La Terrazza Lounge Bar (p43)

Mayday (p44)

Gilli (p44)

Caffè Rivoire (p34)

Amblé (p44)

Getting There

⊁ Walk From Piazza della Stazione walk southeast along Via de' Panzani and Via de' Cerretani to the Duomo. From here, Piazza della Signoria and the Uffizi are a short walk south down Via dei Calzaluoli.

Top Sights
Duomo

Properly titled Cattedrale di Santa Maria del Fiore (Cathedral of St Mary of the Flower), but known as the Duomo (cathedral), this is Florence's iconic landmark. Designed by Sienese architect Arnolfo di Cambio, construction began in 1296 and took almost 150 years. The result – Brunelleschi's distinctive red-tiled cupola, graceful *campanile* (bell tower) and pink, white and green marble facade – is breathtaking.

Cattedrale di Santa Maria del Fiore

👁 Map p36, E1

www.ilgrandemuseodel
duomo.it

Piazza del Duomo

admission free

🕙10am-5pm Mon-Wed & Fri, to 4.30pm Thu, to 4.45pm Sat, 1.30-4.45pm Sun

Duomo interior

Facade

The neo-Gothic facade was designed in the 19th century by architect Emilio de Fabris to replace the uncompleted original. The oldest and most clearly Gothic part of the structure is its south flank, pierced by **Porta dei Canonici** (Canons' Door), a mid-14th-century High Gothic creation (you enter here to climb to the dome).

Cupola

When Michelangelo went to work on St Peter's in Rome, he reportedly said: 'I go to build a greater dome, but not a fairer one', referring to the huge but graceful terracotta-brick **dome** (Brunelleschi's Dome; ☎ 055 230 28 85; www.ilgrandemuseodelduomo.it; Piazza del Duomo; adult/reduced incl cupola, baptistry, campanile, crypt & museum €15/3; ⏱ 8.30am-7pm Mon-Fri, to 5pm Sat, 1-4pm Sun) atop Florence's Duomo. It was constructed between 1420 and 1436 to a design by Filippo Brunelleschi and is a highlight of any visit to Florence.

Interior

After the visual wham-bam of the facade, the sparse decoration of the Duomo's vast interior – 155m long and 90m wide – is a surprise. Most of its artistic treasures have been removed and those that remain are unexpectedly secular, reflecting the fact that the Duomo was built with public funds as a *chiesa di stato* (state church).

Down the left aisle two immense frescoes of equestrian statues portray two *condottieri* (mercenaries) – on the left Niccolò da Tolentino by Andrea del Castagno (1456), and on the right Sir John Hawkwood (who fought in the service of Florence in the 14th century) by Paolo Uccello (1436). In the same aisle, *La Commedia Illumina Firenze* (1465) by Domenico di Michelino depicts poet Dante Alighieri surrounded by the three afterlife worlds

☑ **Top Tips**

▶ Dress code is strict: no shorts, miniskirts or sleeveless tops.

▶ One ticket covers all the sights and is valid for 48 hours (one visit per sight); purchase at www.ilgrandemuseo delduomo.it or at the **ticket office** (⏱ 8.15am-6.45pm), opposite the baptistry entrance at Piazza di San Giovanni 7.

▶ Reservations are obligatory for the Duomo's cupola; book a time slot when buying your ticket online or at a self-service Ticketpoint machine inside the Piazza di San Giovanni ticket office.

✕ **Take a Break**

Post-Duomo, savour modern Tuscan cuisine at contemporary bistro Irene (p40).

Wine bar Coquinarius (p44) is perfect for a dusk-time *aperitivo* with snacks.

he describes in the *Divine Comedy:* purgatory is behind him, his right hand points towards hell, and the city of Florence is paradise.

Clock

Upon entering the Duomo, look up high to see its giant painted clock. One of the first monumental clocks in Europe, it notably turns in an anti-clockwise direction, counts in 24 hours starting at the bottom and begins the first hour of the day at sunset. The clock was painted by Florentine Uccello between 1440 and 1443.

Mass Sacristy

Between the left (north) arm of the transept and the apse is the **Sagrestia delle Messe** (Mass Sacristy), its panelling a marvel of inlaid wood carved by Benedetto and Giuliano da Maiano. The fine bronze doors were executed by Luca della Robbia – his only known work in the material. Above the doorway is his glazed terracotta *Resurrezione* (*Resurrection*).

Crypt of Santa Reparata

A stairway near the Duomo's main entrance leads down to the cathedral gift shop and **Cripta Santa Reparata** (☑ 055 230 28 85; www.ilgrandemuseodel duomo.it; Duomo, Piazza del Duomo; adult/reduced incl cupola, baptistry, campanile, crypt & museum €15/3; ☉ 10am-5pm Mon-Wed & Fri, to 4pm Thu, to 4.45pm Sat), where excavations between 1965 and 1974 unearthed parts of the 5th-century Chiesa di Santa Reparata that originally stood on the site. Pay tribute to architect Filippo Brunelleschi, whose tomb is secreted among the stones here.

Bell Tower

Set next to the Duomo is its slender **campanile** (Bell Tower; Map p36; ☑ 055 230 28 85; www.ilgrandemuseodelduomo. it; Piazza del Duomo; adult/reduced incl campanile, baptistry, cupola, crypt & museum €15/3; ☉ 8.15am-8pm), a striking work of Florentine Gothic architecture designed by Giotto, the artistic genius often described as the founding artist of the Renaissance. The steep 414-step climb up the square, 85m tower offers the reward of a view that is nearly as impressive as that from the dome.

The first tier of bas-reliefs around the base of its elaborate Gothic facade are copies of those carved by Pisano depicting the Creation of Man and the *attività umane* (arts and industries). Those on the second tier depict the planets, the cardinal virtues, the arts and the seven sacraments. The sculpted Prophets and Sibyls in the upper-storey niches are copies of works by Donatello and others.

Baptistry

Across from the Duomo's main entrance is the 11th-century **Battistero di San Giovanni** (Baptistry; Map p36; ☑ 055 230 28 85; www.ilgrandemuseodelduomo. it; Piazza di San Giovanni; adult/reduced incl baptistry, campanile, cupola, crypt & museum €15/3; ☉ 8.15am-10.15am & 11.15am-7.30pm Mon-Fri, 8.15am-6.30pm Sat, 8.15am-1.30pm Sun), an octagonal, striped structure of white-and-green marble. Dante is among the famous people to have been dunked in its baptismal font.

The Romanesque structure is most celebrated, however, for its three sets of doors illustrating the story of humanity and the Redemption. The gilded bronze doors by Lorenzo Ghiberti's at the eastern entrance, the *Porta del Paradiso* (Gate of Paradise), are copies – the originals are in the Grande Museo del Duomo. Andrea Pisano executed the southern doors (1330), illustrating the life of St John the Baptist, and Lorenzo Ghiberti won a public competition in 1401 to design the northern doors, likewise replaced by copies today.

The baptistry's interior gleams with Byzantine-style mosaics. Covering the dome in five horizontal tiers, they include scenes from the lives of St John the Baptist, Christ and Joseph on one side, and a representation of the Last Judgement on the other. A choir of angels surveys proceedings from the innermost tier.

Buy tickets online or at the ticket office at Piazza di San Giovanni 7, opposite the Baptistry entrance.

Grande Museo del Duomo

This awe-inspiring **museum** (Cathedral Museum; Map p36; ☏055 230 28 85; www.ilgrandemuseodelduomo.it; Piazza del Duomo 9; adult/child incl cathedral bell tower, cupola, baptistry & crypt €15/3; ⊙9am-7.30pm)

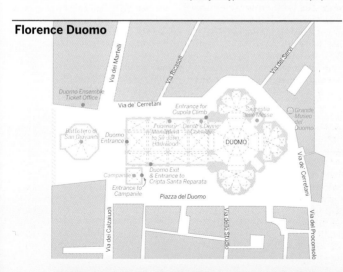

Florence Duomo

DELPIXEL/SHUTTERSTOCK ©

Campanile (bell tower)

tells the magnificent story of how the Duomo and its cupola was built through art and short films.

The museum's spectacular main hall, **Sala del Paradiso**, is dominated by a life-size reconstruction of the original facade of the Duomo, decorated with some forty 14th- and early-15th-century statues carved for the facade by 14th-century masters. Building work began in 1296 but it was never finished and in 1587 the facade was eventually dismantled. This is also where you will find Ghiberti's original 15th-century masterpiece, *Porta del Paradiso* (1425–52; *Doors of Paradise*) – gloriously golden, 16m-tall gilded bronze doors designed for the eastern

entrance to the Baptistry – as well as those he sculpted for the northern entrance (1403–24).

Continuing up to the 1st floor, **Rooms 14 and 15** explain in detail just how Brunelleschi constructed the ground-breaking cathedral dome. Look at 15th-century tools, pulleys, tackles and hoisting wagons used to build the cupola, watch a film and admire Brunelleschi's funeral mask (1446).

Tribuna di Michelangelo

Michelangelo's achingly beautiful *Pietà,* sculpted when he was almost 80 and intended for his own tomb, is displayed here. Dissatisfied with both the quality of the marble and of his own work, Michelangelo broke up the unfinished sculpture, destroying the arm and left leg of the figure of Christ.

Sala del Tresoro

Precious treasures from the Duomo buildings are stashed in the 1st-floor Treasury: don't miss the dazzling altar and monumental cross, crafted from 250kg of pure silver. The twinset was commissioned by Florence's wealthy cloth merchants' guild and executed in 1367 by silversmiths and artists spanning several generations.

Rooftop Terrace

This neighbourhood has ample high points from which to admire Florence's Renaissance splendour: one less known, not to be missed for its larger-than-life cupola views, is the Grande Museo del Duomo's hidden rooftop terrace.

Understand

Scaling Brunelleschi's Dome

One of the finest masterpieces of the Renaissance, the cupola crowning the Duomo is a feat of engineering and one that cannot be fully appreciated without climbing its 463 interior stone steps. Taking his inspiration from Rome's Pantheon, Filippo Brunelleschi (1377–1446) – architect, mathematician, engineer and sculptor – spent an incredible 42 years working on the dome. Starting work in 1419, his mathematical brain and talent for devising innovative engineering solutions enabled him to do what many Florentines had thought impossible: deliver the largest dome to be built in Italy since antiquity.

Brunelleschi arrived at an innovative engineering solution of a distinctive octagonal shape of inner and outer concentric domes resting on the drum of the cathedral rather than the roof itself, allowing artisans to build from the ground up without needing a wooden support frame. Over four million bricks were used in the construction, all of them laid in consecutive rings in horizontal courses using a vertical herringbone pattern.

The climb up the spiral staircase is relatively steep, and should not be attempted if you are claustrophobic. Make sure to pause when you reach the balustrade at the base of the dome, which gives an aerial view of the octagonal *coro* (choir) of the cathedral below and the seven round stained-glass windows (by Donatello, Andrea del Castagno, Paolo Uccello and Lorenzo Ghiberti) that pierce the octagonal drum.

Look up and you'll see the flamboyant late-16th-century frescoes by Giorgio Vasari and Federico Zuccari, depicting the *Giudizio Universale* (*Last Judgement*; 1572–79) and decorating the 4500-sq-m surface of the cupola's inner dome is one of the world's largest paintings. Look for a spent Mother Nature with wrinkled breasts and the four seasons asleep at her feet. Less savoury are the poor souls in hell being sodomised with a pitchfork.

As you climb, snapshots of Florence can be spied through small windows. The final leg – a straight, somewhat hazardous flight up the curve of the inner dome – rewards with an unforgettable 360-degree panorama of one of Europe's most beautiful cities.

Top Sights
Galleria degli Uffizi

Home to the world's greatest collection of Italian Renaissance art, Florence's premier gallery occupies the vast U-shaped Palazzo degli Uffizi. The world-famous collection, displayed in chronological order, spans the gamut of art history from ancient Greek sculpture to 18th-century Venetian paintings.

As part of the ongoing Nuovi Uffizi project, the permanent collection has grown from 45 to 101 revamped rooms; but work remains on temporary-exhibition areas. Expect some halls to be closed, the contents of others changed.

Uffizi Gallery

👁 Map p36, D6

📞 055 29 48 83

www.uffizi.beniculturali.it

Piazzale degli Uffizi 6

adult/reduced €8/4, incl temporary exhibition €12.50/6.25

🕐 8.15am-6.50pm Tue-Sun

Detail of *Madonna con bambino e due angeli*, by Fra' Filippo Lippi

Tuscan 13th-Century Art

Arriving in the **Primo Corridoio** (First Corridor), the first room to the left of the staircase (Room 2) is designed like a medieval chapel to reflect its fabulous contents: three large altarpieces from Florentine churches by Tuscan masters Duccio di Buoninsegna, Cimabue and Giotto. They show the transition from Gothic to nascent Renaissance style.

Sienese 14th-Century Art

The highlight in Room 3 is Simone Martini's shimmering *Annunciazione* (1333), painted with Lippo Memmi and setting the Madonna in a sea of gold. Also of note is *Madonna con il bambino in trono e angeli (Madonna with Child and Saints;* 1340) by Pietro Lorenzetti, which demonstrates a realism similar to Giotto's; unfortunately, both Pietro and his artistic brother Ambrogio died from the plague in Siena in 1348.

Renaissance Pioneers

Perspective was a hallmark of the early-15th-century Florentine school (Room 8) that pioneered the Renaissance. One panel from Paolo Uccello's striking *Battle of San Romano* (1436–40), which celebrates Florence's victory over Siena in 1432, shows the artist's efforts to create perspective with amusing effect as he directs the lances, horses and soldiers to a central disappearing point. In the same room, don't miss the exquisite *Madonna con bambino e due angeli (Madonna and Child with Two Angels;* 1460–65) by Fra' Filippo Lippi, a Carmelite monk who had an unfortunate soft spot for earthly pleasures and scandalously married a nun from Prato. This work clearly influenced his pupil, Sandro Botticelli.

☑ **Top Tips**

▶ Cut out the queue: prebook tickets online (reservation €4) and collect on arrival.

▶ Check the latest new rooms (and those temporarily closed during expansion works) in the 'News' section of www.uffizi.org.

▶ Dress light: leave bags in the ground-floor wardrobe by the main entrance, but you are obliged to carry your coat around with you.

▶ Allow time to linger in the 2nd-floor Secondo Corridoio (Second Corridor) linking the Primo (First) and Terzo (Third) corridors – views of the Arno and Florentine hills beyond are intoxicating.

✕ **Take a Break**

Head to the Uffizi's rooftop cafe for fresh air and fabulous views.

Lunch on gourmet *panini* (sandwiches), wine and Tuscan chocolate at 'Ino (p42).

Duke & Duchess of Urbino

Revel in the realism of Piero della Francesca's 1465 warts-and-all portraits of the Duke and Duchess of Urbino (Room 9). The crooked-nosed duke lost his right eye in a jousting accident, hence the focus on his left side only, while the duchess is deathly stone-white to convey the fact that the portrait was painted posthumously.

Botticelli

The spectacular **Sala del Botticelli**, numbered 10 to 14 but really two light and graceful rooms, is always packed. Of the 18 Botticelli works displayed in the Uffizi in all, his iconic *La nascita di Venere* (*The Birth of Venus;* c 1485), *Primavera* (*Spring;* c 1482) and *Madonna del Magnificat* (*Madonna of the Magnificat;* 1483) are the best-known works by the Renaissance master known for his ethereal figures. Take time to study the lesser known *Annunciazione* (Annunciation), a 6m-wide fresco painted by Botticelli in 1481 for the San Martino hospital in Florence. True aficionados rate his twin set of miniatures depicting a sword-bearing Judith returning from the camp of Holofernes and the discovery of the decapitated Holofernes in his tent (1495–1500) as being among his finest works.

The Tribune

The Medici clan stashed away their most precious art in this octagonal-shaped treasure trove (Room 18),

Uffizi Gallery

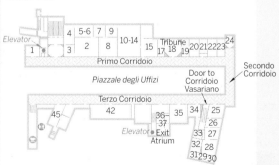

Second Floor

created by Francesco I between 1581 and 1586. Designed to amaze, it features a small collection of classical statues and paintings on its upholstered silk walls and 6000 crimson-varnished mother-of-pearl shells encrusting the domed ceiling.

Michelangelo

Michelangelo's dazzling *Doni Tondo,* a depiction of the Holy Family, hangs in Room 35. The composition is unusual and the colours as vibrant as when they were first applied in 1504–06. It was painted for wealthy Florentine merchant Agnolo Doni (who hung it above his bed) and bought by the Medici for Palazzo Pitti in 1594.

Madonna of the Goldfinch

Downstairs in the 1st-floor galleries, Rooms 46 to 55 display 16th- to 18th-century works by foreign artists, including Rembrandt (Room 49), Rubens and Van Dyck (who share Room 55), Andrea del Sarto (Rooms 57 and 58) and Raphael (Room 66), whose *Madonna del cardellino (Madonna of the Goldfinch;* 1505–06) steals the show. Raphael painted it during his four-year sojourn in Florence.

Medici Portraits

Room 65 showcases Agnolo Bronzino (1503–72), official portrait artist at the court of Cosimo I. His 1545 portraits of the Grand Duchess Eleonora of Toledo and her son Giovanni together, and the 18-month-old Giovanni alone holding a goldfinch – symbolising his calling into the church – are masterpieces of 16th-century European portraiture.

Leonardo da Vinci

Four early Florentine works by Leonardo da Vinci are currently displayed in Room 79. (In due course, Leonardo could well be shifted back upstairs to the 2nd floor.) His *Annunciazione* (*Annunciation;* 1472) was deliberately painted to be admired, not face on, but rather from the lower right-hand side of the painting. In spring 2017, one of Da Vinci's most dazzling early works, the partly unfinished *Adorazione dei Magi* (*Adoration of the Magi;* 1481–82), returned to the Uffizi after six lengthy years of intricate restoration.

Caravaggio

Room 90, with its canary-yellow walls, features works by Caravaggio, deemed vulgar at the time for his direct interpretation of reality. The *Head of Medusa* (1598–99), commissioned for a ceremonial shield, is supposedly a self-portrait of the young artist who died at the age of 39. The biblical drama of an angel steadying the hand of Abraham as he holds a knife to his son Isaac's throat in Caravaggio's *Sacrifice of Isaac* (1601–02) is glorious in its intensity.

Local Life
A Boutique Shopping Spree

Florence is naturally stylish – the city did spawn the Renaissance and Gucci after all – which translates as world-class shopping. Big-name fashion designers bejewel Florence's smartest shopping strip, Via de' Tornabuoni, but it is the small independent boutiques squirrelled away in the ancient maze of narrow, cobbled lanes around the Duomo and Piazza della Signoria that really enchant.

❶ Morning Coffee at Rivoire

Nudge your shopping spirit into gear with a coffee or cup of the city's most decadent hot chocolate on the people-watching terrace of **Caffè Rivoire** (☎ 055 21 44 12; www.rivoire.it; Piazza della Signoria 4; ⏲ 7am-midnight Tue-Sun summer, to 9pm winter), a historic cafe dating to 1872. Join Florentines standing at the bar (rather than sitting at a table).

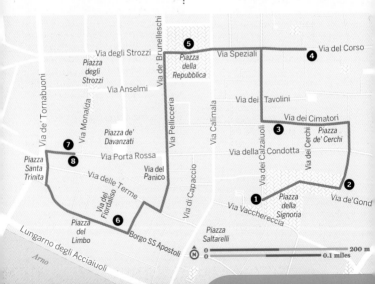

2 A Date with Gucci

Cross the square on which Savonarola set fire to the city's art – books, paintings, musical instruments, mirrors, fine clothes – during his famous 'Bonfire of the Vanities' in 1497 and pop into **Gucci Museo** (www.gucci.com; Piazza della Signoria 10; adult/reduced €7/5; ⏱10am-8pm, to 11pm Fri). The museum, with fashionable icon store attached, illustrates the story of the Gucci fashion house, from its first luggage pieces to the present day.

3 Benheart

Men's and women's shoes to die for, double-lined with soft buffalo leather and stitched before being dyed with natural pigments, steal the show at the **flagship store** (☎055 046 26 38; www.benheart.it; Via dei Cimatori 25r; ⏱10am-8pm) of local superstar fashion designer, Ben. He set up business with Florentine schoolmate Matteo after undergoing a heart transplant.

4 Fabriano Boutique

Luxurious writing paper, origami and pop-up greeting cards entice customers into this thoroughly modern **stationery boutique** (☎055 28 51 94; www.fabrianoboutique.com; Via del Corso 59r; ⏱9am-7.30pm) – a refreshing change from the traditional norm. Watch for occasional card-making, calligraphy and origami workshops.

5 Piazza della Repubblica

On the old Roman forum, take a coffee break with Florentines in **La Terrazza** (La Rinascente, Piazza della Repubblica 1; ⏱9am-9pm Mon-Sat, 10.30am-8pm Sun), on the 5th floor of the city's local department store, and swoon over the sterling city panorama that unfolds from its 'secret' rooftop terrace.

6 Angela Caputi

Florentines adore the bold, colourful resin jewellery of **Angela Caputi** (☎055 29 29 93; www.angelacaputi.com; Borgo SS Apostoli 42-46; ⏱10am-1pm & 3.30-7.30pm Mon-Sat), at work in Florence since the 1970s. Eye-catching costume gems and jewels are her forté, shown off to perfection against one-of-a-kind women's fashion labels uncovered during her worldwide travels.

7 Il Papiro

One of several branches around town, this elegant **boutique** (☎055 21 65 93; http://ilpapirofirenze.eu/en/; Via Porta Rosso 76; ⏱10am-7pm) sells books, journals, writing paper, cards and other stationery made from Florence's signature, hand-decorated marbled paper – the perfect gift to take back home.

8 A Third-Generation Silversmith

Florence's third-generation **Pampaloni** (☎055 28 90 94; www.pampaloni.com; Via Porta Rossa 97; ⏱10am-1.30pm & 3-7.30pm Mon-Sat) silver shop, born out of a tiny workshop on Ponte Vecchio in 1902, is the epitome of elegance with its sleek silver collections for the table and home, and contemporary silver jewellery.

Piazza San Firenze

Borgo dei Greci

Via del Corno

Via Vinegia

Via de' Neri

Piazza Mentana

Via de'Gondi

Via de' Leoni

Via del Grano

Piazza degli Uffizi

Piazza del Grano

1 ❶ Palazzo Vecchio

Piazza Castellani

Via de'Castellani

Via del Castello d'Altafronte

Via dei Saponai

Lungarno Generale Diaz

Piazza 5 ❶ della Signoria

Galleria degli Uffizi

Piazzale degli Uffizi

Museo Galileo 8 ❶

Piazza de' Giudici

Via Calimaruzza

Piazza di Santa Cecilia

Via Vacchereccia

Chiasso de' Baroncelli

Uffizi Ticket Office

Via Calima

Via di Capaccio

Via Lambertesca

Piazza Saltarelli

Via Por Santa Maria

Chiesa di Santo Stefano

Via de' Girolami

Via dei Georgofili

12 ❌

Corridoio Vasariano 2 ❶

Arno

Piazza dei Giudici

Lungarno Torrigiani

Via de' Bardi

Chiasso di Manetto

Vic. dell'Oro

Piazza de' Santo Stefano

Piazza de' Santo Stefano

Corridoio Vasariano

Costa di San Giorgio

Cde Davizi

Chiasso delle Misure

15 ❌

17 ❶

Piazza dei Rossi

Piazza Santa Felicità

Via delle Terme

Chiasso del Cornino

Borgo SS Apostoli

Ponte Vecchio

Via Stracciatella

Via de' Bardi

Vicolo della Cava

Via del Fiordaliso

20 ❶
27 ❶

Lungarno degli Acciaiuoli

Piazza del Limbo 29 ❶

Borgo San Jacopo

Via de' Barbadori

Borgo San Jacopo

Via Guicciardini

Santa Trinità

Via de' Ramaglianti

5

6

7

8

E

D

C

B

A

Sights

Palazzo Vecchio
MUSEUM

1 Map p36, D5

This fortress palace, with its crenellations and 94m-high tower, was designed by Arnolfo di Cambio between 1298 and 1314 for the *signoria* (city government). It remains the seat of the city's power, home to the mayor's office and the municipal council. From the top of the **Torre d'Arnolfo** (tower), you can revel in unforgettable rooftop views. Inside, Michelangelo's *Genio della Vittoria* (*Genius of Victory*) sculpture graces the Salone dei Cinquecento, a magnificent painted hall created for the city's 15th-century ruling Consiglio dei Cinquecento (Council of 500). (☑ 055 27 68 22, 055 276 85 58; www.musefirenze.it; Piazza della Signoria; adult/reduced museum €10/8, tower €10/8, museum & tower €14/12, archaeological tour €4, combination ticket €18/16; ☺ museum 9am-11pm Fri-Wed, to 2pm Thu Apr-Sep, 9am-7pm Fri-Wed, to 2pm Thu Oct-Mar, tower 9am-9pm Fri-Wed, to 2pm Thu Apr-Sep, 10am-5pm Fri-Wed, to 2pm Thu Oct-Mar)

Corridoio Vasariano
BRIDGE

2 Map p36, C7

This 1km-long covered passageway connects Palazzo Vecchio with the Uffizi (p30) and Palazzo Pitti (p100). It was designed by Vasari in 1565 to allow the Medici to wander between their palaces in privacy and comfort. In the 17th century the Medici strung it with hundreds of artworks, including self-

 Top Tip

Palazzo Vecchio Tours

To get the most out of one of Florence's most dynamic, well-thought-out museums, join one of its excellent guided tours or hands-on workshops that take you into parts of Palazzo Vecchio that are otherwise inaccessible. Many are in English; you need a valid museum ticket in addition to the guided-tour ticket. Reserve in advance by telephone, email info@muse.comune.fi.it or directly at the **Firenze Musei** (http://musefirenze.it) ticket desk inside Palazzo Vecchio.

portraits of Andrea del Sarto, Rubens, Rembrandt and Canova. Closed for renovation in 2017, the Vasarian Corridor will be open to guided tours once work is complete; contact **Florence Town** (☑ 055 28 11 03; www.florencetown.com; Via de' Lamberti 1) or **Caf Tour & Travel** (☑ 055 28 32 00; www.caftours.com; Via degli Alfani 151r; ☺ 7.30am-8pm Mon-Sat, to 5pm Sun). (Vasarian Corridor; ☺ by guided tour; 🚇 B)

Museo di Palazzo Davanzati
MUSEUM

3 Map p36, B4

This is the address to see precisely how Florentine nobles lived in the 16th century. Home to the wealthy Davanzati merchant family from 1578, this 14th-century *palazzo* (mansion) with a wonderful central loggia, is a gem. Peep at the carved faces of the original owners on the pillars in the inner courtyard and don't miss the 1st-floor **Sala Madornale** (Reception Room) with its painted wooden ceiling, exotic **Sala dei Pappagalli** (Parrot Room) and **Camera dei Pavoni** (Peacock Bedroom). (☑055 238 86 10; www.polomuseale.firenze.it; Via Porta Rossa 13; adult/reduced €6/3; ⊙8.15am-2pm, closed 1st, 3rd & 5th Mon, 2nd & 4th Sun of month)

Chiesa e Museo di Orsanmichele
CHURCH, MUSEUM

4 ◉ Map p36, C4

This unusual and inspirational church, with a Gothic tabernacle by Andrea Orcagna, was created when the arcades of an old grain market (1290) were walled in and two storeys added during the 14th century. Its exterior is decorated with niches and tabernacles bearing statues. Representing the patron saints of Florence's many guilds, the statues were commissioned in the 15th and 16th centuries after the *signoria* ordered the city's guilds to finance the church's decoration. (☑055 21 58 52; Via dell'Arte della Lana; admission free; ⊙museum 10am-5pm Mon, church 10am-5pm daily, closed Mon Aug)

Piazza della Signoria
PIAZZA

5 ◉ Map p36, D5

The hub of local life since the 13th century, Florentines flock here to meet friends and chat over early-evening *aperitivi* at historic cafes. Presiding over everything is Palazzo Vecchio (p38), Florence's city hall, and the

Palazzo Vecchio

14th-century **Loggia dei Lanzi** (admission free), an open-air gallery showcasing Renaissance sculptures, including Giambologna's *Rape of the Sabine Women* (c 1583), Benvenuto Cellini's bronze *Perseus* (1554) and Agnolo Gaddi's *Seven Virtues* (1384–89). (Piazza della Signoria)

Piazza della Repubblica
PIAZZA

6 ◉ Map p36, C3

The site of a Roman forum and heart of medieval Florence, this busy civic space was created in the 1880s as part of a controversial plan of 'civic improvements' involving the demolition of the old market, Jewish ghetto and

Local Life
Le Passeggiata

Nothing is more sacrosanct than the early-evening stroll; follow Florentines to **Via de' Tornabuoni**, the city's most expensive shopping strip nicknamed the 'Salotto di Firenze' (Florence's Drawing Room). Renaissance palaces and Italian fashion houses border each side of the elegant, car-free strip, making it prime terrain to don suitable dress and walk, chat and smooch in chic company. End with a bite-sized truffle *panini* and flute of sparkling *prosecco* at 19th-century English pharmacy-turned-genteel cafe Procacci (p46).

slums, and the relocation of nearly 6000 residents. Vasari's lovely Loggia del Pesce (Fish Market) was saved and re-erected on Via Pietrapiana.

Palazzo Strozzi

GALLERY

 7 Map p36, A3

This 15th-century Renaissance mansion was built for wealthy merchant Filippo Strozzi, one of the Medici's major political and commercial rivals. Today, it hosts exciting art exhibitions. There's always a buzz about the place, with young Florentines congregating in the courtyard **Caffé Strozzi** (☏055 28 82 36; www.strozzicaffe.com; Piazza degli Strozzi 1; ⏲8am-8.30pm Mon, to 1am Tue-Sun; 🛜). Art workshops, tours and other activities aimed squarely at families make the gallery a firm favourite with pretty much everyone.

(☏055 246 96 00; www.palazzostrozzi.org; Piazza degli Strozzi; adult/reduced €12/9.50, family ticket €22; ⏲10am-8pm Tue, Wed & Fri-Sun, to 11pm Thu)

Museo Galileo

MUSEUM

 8 Map p36, D7

On the river next to the Uffizi in 12th-century Palazzo Castellani – look for the sundial telling the time on the pavement outside – is this state-of-the-art science museum, named after the great Pisa-born scientist Galileo Galilei, who was invited by the Medici court to Florence in 1610 (don't miss two of his fingers and a tooth displayed here). (☏055 26 53 11; www.museogalileo.it; Piazza dei Giudici 1; adult/reduced €9/5.50; ⏲9.30am-6pm Wed-Mon, to 1pm Tue)

Eating

Irene

BISTRO €€€

9 Map p36, C3

Named after the accomplished Italian grandmother of Sir Rocco Forte of the same-name luxury hotel group, Irene (actually part of neighbouring Hotel Savoy) is a dazzling contemporary bistro with a pavement terrace (heated in winter) overlooking iconic Piazza della Repubblica. Interior design is retro-chic 1950s and celebrity chef Fulvio Pierangelini cooks up a playful, utterly fabulous bistro cuisine in his Tuscan kitchen. (☏055 273 58 91; www.roccofortehotels.com; Piazza della Repubblica 7; meals €60; ⏲12.30-10.30pm)

Osteria Il Buongustai

OSTERIA €

10 Map p36, D4

Run with breathtaking speed and grace by Laura and Lucia, this place is unmissable. Lunchtimes heave with locals who work nearby and savvy students who flock here to fill up on tasty Tuscan home cooking at a snip of other restaurant prices. The place is brilliantly no frills – expect to share a table and pay in cash; no credit cards. (☎055 29 13 04; Via dei Cerchi 15r; meals €15-20; ⏰8am-4pm Mon-Fri, to 11pm Sat)

Trattoria Le Mossacce

TRATTORIA €

11 Map p36, E3

Strung with legs of ham and garlic garlands, this old-world trattoria lives up to its vintage promise of a warm *benvenuto* (welcome) and fabulous home cooking every Tuscan Nonna would approve of. A family address, it has been the pride and joy of the Fantoni-Mannucci family for the last 50-odd years and their *bistecca alla fiorentina* (T-bone steak) is among the best in town. (☎055 29 43 61; www.trattoria lemossacce.it; Via del Proconsolo 55r; meals €20; ⏰noon-2.30pm & 7-9.30pm Mon-Fri)

Understand

Backstreet Florence: Dante

Italy's most divine poet was born in 1265 in a wee house down a narrow lane in the backstreets of Florence. Tragic romance made him tick and there's no better place to unravel the medieval life and times of Dante than the **Museo Casa di Dante** (☎055 21 94 16; Via Santa Margherita 1; adult/reduced €4/2; ⏰10am-5pm Mon-Fri, 10am-6pm Sat & Sun).

When Dante was just 12 he was promised in marriage to Gemma Donati. But it was another Florentine gal, Beatrice Portinari (1266–90), who was his muse, his inspiration, the love of his life (despite only ever meeting her twice in his life).

Beatrice, who wed a banker and died a couple of years later aged just 24, is buried in 11th-century **Chiesa di Santa Margherita** (Via Santa Margherita 4; ⏰hours vary), in an alley near Dante's house; note the wicker basket in front of her grave filled with scraps of paper on which prayers and dedications evoking unrequited love have been penned. This chapel was also where the poet married Gemma in 1295. Dimly lit, it remains much as it was in medieval Florence.

Local Life

Tripe Carts

When Florentines fancy a munch-on-the-move, they flit by a *trippaio* – a cart on wheels or mobile stand – for a tripe *panini* (sandwich). Think cow's stomach chopped up, boiled, sliced, seasoned and bunged between bread.

Those great bastions of good old-fashioned Florentine tradition still going strong include **Il Trippaio del Porcellino** (☎ 335 8070240; Piazza del Mercato Nuovo 1; tripe €4.50; ⊗9am-6.30pm Mon-Sat) and hole-in-the-wall **Da Vinattieri** (Map p36, E3; Via Santa Margherita 4; panini €4.50; ⊗10am-7.30pm Mon-Fri, to 8pm Sat & Sun). Pay €4.50 for a *panini* with tripe doused in *salsa verde* (pea-green sauce of smashed parsley, garlic, capers and anchovies) or order a bowl of *lampredotto* (cow's fourth stomach, chopped and simmered).

'Ino
SANDWICHES €

12   Map p36, C6

Artisan ingredients sourced locally and mixed creatively by passionate gourmet Alessandro Frassica is the secret behind this gourmet sandwich bar near the Uffizi. Create your own *panino* combo, pick from dozens of fun house specials, or go for an enticingly topped bruschetta instead – in the grand company of a glass of Tuscan wine or craft beer. (☎ 055 21 45 14; www.inofirenze.com; Via dei Georgofili 3r-7r; bruschette/panini €6/8; ⊗noon-4.30pm)

Grom
GELATO €

13   Map p36, D2

Rain, hail or shine, queues run halfway down the street at this sweet address; many ingredients are organic. Tasty hot chocolate and milkshakes, too. (☎ 055 21 61 58; www.grom.it; Via del Campanile 2; cones €2.60-4.60; tubs €2.60-5.50; ⊗10am-10.30pm Sun-Thu, to 11.30pm Fri & Sat)

Cantinetta dei Verrazzano
TUSCAN €

14   Map p36, D4

A *forno* (baker's oven) and *cantinetta* (small cellar) make a heavenly match in foodie Florence. Sit down at a marble-topped table, sip your pick of wine from the Verrazzano family's 52-hectare estate in Greve in Chianti, and tuck into traditional focaccia, *cecina* (chickpea bread) or a mixed salami platter – the *sbriciolona* (fennel seed salami) is not to be missed. (☎ 055 26 85 90; www.verrazzano.com; Via dei Tavolini 18-20; focaccia from €3; ⊗8am-9pm Mon-Sat, 10am-9pm Sun)

Mangiafoco
TUSCAN €€

15   Map p36, B5

Aromatic truffles get full-page billing at this small and cosy *osteria* (casual tavern) with buttercup-yellow walls, cushioned seating and an exceptional wine list. Whether you are a hardcore truffle fiend or a virgin, there is something for you here: steak topped with freshly shaved truffles in season, truffle *taglietelle* (ribbon pasta) or a

Grom

simple plate of mixed cheeses with sweet truffle honey. (☎055 265 81 70; www.mangiafoco.com; Borgo SS Apostoli 26r; meals €40; ⏱10am-10pm Mon-Sat)

Obicà
ITALIAN €€

16 Map p36, A3

Given its exclusive location in Palazzo Tornabuoni, this designer address is naturally uber-trendy – even the table mats are upcycled from organic products. Taste 10 different types of mozzarella cheese in the cathedral-like interior or snuggle beneath heaters over pizza and salads on sofas in the enchanting star-topped courtyard. At *aperitivo* hour nibble on *taglierini*

(tasting boards loaded with cheeses, salami, deep-fried veg). (☎055 277 35 26; www.obica.com; Via de' Tornabuoni 16; meals €30-50; ⏱noon-4pm & 6.30-11.30pm Mon-Fri, noon-11pm Sat & Sun)

Drinking

La Terrazza Lounge Bar
BAR

17  Map p36, B6

This rooftop bar with wooden-decking terrace accessible from the 5th floor of the 1950s-styled, design Hotel Continentale is as chic as one would expect of a fashion-house hotel. Its *aperitivo* buffet is a modest affair, but

Local Life
The Finest Ice in Town

Known throughout Italy for the quality of its handmade gelato and sweet pastries, **Gelateria Pasticceria Badiani** (☎055 57 86 82; www. buontalenti.it; Viale dei Mille 20r; ☺7am-1am summer, to midnight Sun-Thu, to 1am Fri & Sat winter) is located in the Campo de' Marte neighbourhood just outside the historic city centre but is – as any local will tell you – well worth the walk. The house speciality is Buontalenti gelato, a creamy concoction with flavourings that are a heavily guarded house secret.

who cares with that fabulous, drop-dead-gorgeous panorama of one of Europe's most beautiful cities. Dress the part, or feel out of place. Count on €19 for a cocktail. (☎055 2726 5987; www.lungarnocollection.com; Vicolo dell' Oro 6r; ☺2.30-11.30pm Apr-Sep)

Mayday
COCKTAIL BAR

18 Map p36, D4

Strike up a conversation with passionate mixologist Marco at Mayday. Within seconds you'll be hooked on his homemade mixers and astonishing infusions, all handmade using wholly Tuscan ingredients. Think pancetta-infused whisky, saffron *limoncello* (lemon liqueur) and porcini liqueur. Marco's cocktail list is equally impressive – or tell him your favourite flavours and let yourself be surprised.

(☎055 238 12 90; Via Dante Alighieri 16; cocktails €8; ☺7pm-2am Tue-Sat)

Gilli
CAFE

19 Map p36, C3

The most famous of the historic cafes on the city's old Roman forum, Gilli has been serving utterly delectable cakes, chocolates, fruit tartlets and *millefoglie* (sheets of puff pastry filled with rich vanilla or chocolate Chantilly cream) to die for since 1733 (it moved to this square in 1910 and sports a beautifully preserved art nouveau interior). (☎055 21 38 96; www.gilli.it; Piazza della Repubblica 39r; ☺7.30am-1.30am)

Amblé
BAR

20 Map p36, B6

You need to know about this cafe-bar, near Ponte Vecchio, to find it. Vintage furniture – all for sale – creates a hip, shabby-chic vibe and the tiny terrace feels delightfully far from the madding crowd on summer evenings. From the river, head down Vicolo dell' Oro to the Hotel Continentale, and turn left along the alleyway that runs parallel to the river. (☎055 26 85 28; Piazzetta dei del Bene 7a; ☺10am-midnight Tue-Sat, noon-midnight Sun)

Coquinarius
WINE BAR

21 Map p36, D2

With its old stone vaults, scrubbed wooden tables and refreshingly modern air, this *enoteca* run by the dynamic Nicolas is spacious and stylish. The wine list features bags of Tuscan

Understand

Florentine Artists

In many respects, the history of Florentine art is also the history of Western art. Browse through any text on the subject and you'll quickly develop an understanding of how influential the Italian Renaissance, which kicked off and reached its greatest flowering here, has been over the past 500 years. Indeed, it's no exaggeration to say that architecture, painting and sculpture rely on its technical innovations and take inspiration from its Humanist subject matter to this very day.

Of the many artists who trained, worked and lived in the city, the most famous are Giotto di Bondone (c 1266–1337), Donatello (c 1386–1466), Fra' Angelico (c 1395–1455), Masaccio (1401–28), Filippo Lippi (c 1406–69), Benozzo Gozzoli (c 1421–97), Sandro Botticelli (1445–1510), Domenico Ghirlandaio (1449–94) and Michelangelo Buonarroti (1475–1564).

The city is full of artistic masterpieces – in fact, Florence itself is often described as the world's biggest and most spectacular museum. It's impossible to see everything in one trip, but the **Uffizi Gallery** should be every visitor's first stop. Its peerless collection contains major works by every Renaissance artist of note, with Botticelli's *Primavera*, *Birth of Venus*, *Cestello Annunciation* and *Adoration of the Magi* being four of the gallery's best-loved works (Michelangelo's *Tondo Doni* is another).

Sculptures abound – most notably Michelangelo's *David* in the **Galleria dell'Accademia** – but the greatest and most significant concentration of works can be found in the **Museo del Bargello**, home to Donatello's two versions of *David* (one marble, the other bronze) and a number of works by Michelangelo.

Frescoing was an important artistic technique in the Renaissance, and Florentine churches are rich repositories of these murals painted on freshly laid lime plaster. Head to **Basilica di Santa Maria Novella** to see Ghirlandaio's wonderful examples in the Cappella Maggiore; the **Museo di San Marco** to see those of Fra' Angelico (including his deeply spiritual *Annunciation*); the **Cappella Brancacci** to see Masaccio's oft-reproduced *Expulsion of Adam and Eve from Paradise;* and the **Palazzo Medici-Riccardi** to admire Benozzo Gozzoli's charming *Procession of the Magi to Bethlehem.*

Local Life

Aperitivi

Join locals for summertime early-evening cocktails on the chic rooftop terrace of La Terrazza Lounge Bar (p43) or the back-alley garden of shabby-chic Amblé (p44). Winter or summer, stylish Irene (p40), with a box terrace on Piazza della Repubblica, is an *aperitivo* hot spot.

greats and unknowns, and outstanding crostini and *carpacci* (cold sliced meats) ensure you don't leave hungry. The ravioli stuffed with silky *burrata* cheese and smothered in pistachio pesto is particularly outstanding. (www.coquinarius.com; Via delle Oche 11r; ⏱12.30-3pm & 6.30-10.30pm Wed-Mon)

Procacci

CAFE, BAR

22 Map p36, A3

The last remaining bastion of genteel old Florence on Via de' Tornabuoni, this tiny cafe was born in 1885 opposite an English pharmacy as a delicatessen serving truffles in its repertoire of tasty morsels. Bite-sized *panini tartufati* (truffle pâté rolls) remain the thing to order, best accompanied by a glass of *prosecco* (sparkling wine). (☎055 21 16 56; www.procacci1885.it; Via de' Tornabuoni 64r; ⏱10am-9pm Mon-Sat, 11am-8pm Sun, closed 3 weeks Aug)

Fiaschetteria Nuvoli

WINE BAR

23 Map p36, C1

Pull up a stool on the street and chat with a regular over a glass of *vino della casa* (house wine) at this old-fashioned *fiaschetteria* (wine seller), a street away from the Duomo. Food, too. (☎055 239 66 16; Piazza dell'Olio 15r; ⏱8am-9pm Mon-Sat)

Shake Café

CAFE

24 Map p36, D3

Smoothie bowls with protein powder, kale and goji berries, cold-pressed juices and vitamin-packed elixir shots – to eat in or take away – satisfy wellness cravings at this laid-back cafe on people-busy Via del Corso. International newspapers, mellow music and a relaxed vibe make it a hipster place to hang. All-day wraps, salads and hearty, homemade soups (€6 to €7.50), too. (☎055 21 59 52; www.shakecafe.bio; Via del Corso 28-32; ⏱7.30am-8pm)

YAB

CLUB

25 Map p36, B4

Pick your night according to your age and tastes at this hugely popular nightclub with electric dance floor, around since the 1970s, behind Palazzo Strozzi. (☎055 21 51 60; www.yab.it/en; Via de' Sassetti 5r; ⏱7pm-4am Mon & Wed-Sat Oct-May)

MICHELE BUZZI/SHUTTERSTOCK ©

Fiaschetteria Nuvoli

Shopping

A Piedi Nudi nel Parco
FASHION & ACCESSORIES

26 🔒 Map p36, E4

Specialising in high-end avant-garde designers for women, this boutique is so chic that it even has a tiny bar serving *aperitivi* (from 6pm) while you shop. (🏴055 21 80 99; www.pnp-firenze. com; Via del Proconsolo 1; ⏰10.30am-7.30pm Mon-Sat, noon-7.30pm Sun)

Boutique Nadine
FASHION & ACCESSORIES

27 🔒 Map p36, B6

For exquisite vintage clothing, jewellery, ornaments and stylish knick-knacks for the home, browse this old-world boutique on the riverside near Ponte Vecchio. Find the original, larger branch (p89) in Santa Croce. (🏴055 28 78 51; Lungarno degli Acciaiuoli 22r; ⏰2.30-7.30pm Mon, 10am-7.30pm Tue-Sat)

Patrizia Pepe
FASHION & ACCESSORIES

28 🔒 Map p36, C2

Modern, colourful designs for women and children are the signature of this Florentine fashion house, created in 1993 by creative spirit Patrizia Bambi and business partner, Claudio Orrea. A bit rock chic, a bit wild child, Patrizia Pepe never fails to thrill. (🏴055 264 50 56; www.patriziapepe.com; Piazza di San Giovanni 12r; ⏰9am-8pm)

La Bottega dell'Olio
FOOD

29 🔒 Map p36, A5

This bijou boutique takes great care with its displays of olive oils, olive-oil soaps, platters made from olive wood and skincare products made with olive oil (the Lepo range is particularly good). (🏴055 267 04 68; www. labottegadelloliofirenze.it; Piazza del Limbo 4r; ⏰2.30-6.30pm Mon, 10am-1pm & 2-6.30pm Tue-Sat)

Explore

Santa Maria Novella

Anchored by its magnificent basilica, this ancient and intriguing part of Florence defies easy description – from the rough-cut streets around the station it's only a short walk to the busy social scene around recently gentrified Piazza di Santa Maria Novella and the hip boutiques on the atmosphere-laden 'backstreets' west of elegant Via de' Tornabuoni.

The Sights in a Day

☼ Enjoy one of Florence's finest cappuccinos at mythical **Caffè Giacosa** (p57) amid the prework hub-bub of smartly dressed Florentines downing espresso shots at the bar. Meander north to the monumental hulk of **Basilica di Santa Maria Novella** (p50). Spend the morning exploring the sacred complex and its Renais-sance frescoes. End the morning with an antidote of modern art at **Museo Novecento** (p54).

☼ Lunch light and local at **Mariano** (p56), a wine bar with made-to-measure *panini* (sandwiches). Eat in with a glass of wine or wander to the Arno for a picnic with Ponte Vecchio views. Afterwards, admire bril-liant frescoes inside **Chiesa di Santa Trìnita** (p55).

☾ Give your credit card an after-noon workout in the fashion boutiques west of Via de' Tornabuoni (pictured left): old-world Via della Spada enjoys the added lure of the startling Cappella Rucellai inside **Museo Marino Marini** (p54). Shop for sweetly fragranced, take-home gifts at **Officina Profumo-Farmaceutica di Santa Maria Novella** (p59) then hit **Sei Divino** (p58) for an *aperitivo* (pre-dinner drink). Dine on traditional Tus-can fare at **Trattoria Marione** (p56).

◉ Top Sight

Basilica di Santa Maria Novella (p50)

♥ Best of Florence

Shopping
La Bottega Della Frutta (p59)

Officina Profumo-Farmaceutica di Santa Maria Novella (p59)

Mio Concept (p59)

Letizia Fiorini (p60)

Pineider (p60)

Dolceforte (p60)

Eating
Trattoria Marione (p56)

Mariano (p56)

Drinking
Caffè Giacosa (p57)

Todo Modo (p57)

Getting There

🚶 **Walk** From Piazza della Stazi-one turn south into Via degli Avelli and you will almost immediately come to Piazza di Santa Maria No-vella and its magnificent basilica.

Top Sights
Basilica di Santa Maria Novella

This monastery complex, fronted by the striking green-and-white marble facade of its basilica, hides romantic church cloisters and a stunning frescoed chapel behind its monumental walls. The basilica itself is a treasure chest of artistic masterpieces, climaxing with frescoes by Domenico Ghirlandaio and a luminous painted *Crucifix* by Giotto (c 1290).

⊙ Map p52, G2

☏ 055 21 92 57

www.smn.it

Piazza di Santa Maria Novella 18

adult/reduced €5/3.50

⊘ 9am-7pm Mon-Thu, 11am-7pm Fri, 9am-6.30pm Sat, noon-6.30pm Sun summer, shorter hours winter

Cappella Maggiore

Holy Trinity

As you enter, look straight ahead to see Masaccio's superb fresco *Holy Trinity* (1424–25), one of the first artworks to use the then newly discovered techniques of perspective and proportion.

Cappella Maggiore

Look behind the main altar to find this tiny chapel adorned in vibrant frescoes by Ghirlandaio between 1485 and 1490. Relating the lives of the Virgin Mary, the frescoes are notable for their depiction of Florentine life during the Renaissance. Spot portraits of the Tornabuoni family who commissioned the frescoes.

Cappella Strozzi di Mantova

To the far left of the altar, up a short flight of stairs, is this wonderful chapel covered in soul-stirring 14th-century frescoes by Niccolò di Tommaso and Nardo di Cione. The fine altarpiece (1354–57) here was painted by the latter's brother, Andrea, better known as Andrea Orcagna.

Chiostro Verde

The serenely beautiful Green Cloister (1332–62) is named after the green earth base used for the frescoes on three of its four walls. On its west side, another passage leads to 14th-century **Cappella degli Ubriachi** and a refectory (1353–54) featuring ecclesiastical relics and a 1583 *Last Supper* by Alessandro Allori.

Cappellone degli Spagnoli

A door off the cloister's northern side leads into this chapel, named in 1566 when it was given to the Spanish colony in Florence (Spagnoli means Spanish). Its extraordinary frescoes (c 1365–67) by Andrea di Bonaiuto depict the *Resurrection*, *Ascension* and *Pentecost* (vault); on the altar wall are scenes of the *Via Dolorosa*, *Crucifixion* and *Descent into Limbo*.

☑ Top Tips

▶ Allow at least two hours to take it all in; book highly recommended guided tours (€4, 1¼ hours) through Firenze Musei (p182) or directly at the museum.

▶ Watch out for major expansion work at the complex that will open the Chiostro Grande (Big Cloister) and Cappella del Papa to visitors; the old dormitories will become a new reception area, bookshop and cafe.

✕ Take a Break

Freshen up with a herbal infusion at Officina Profumo-Farmaceutica di Santa Maria Novella (p59), a 17th-century pharmacy-boutique with tearoom where monks from Santa Maria Novella concocted herbal remedies in the 17th century.

The marble steps leading up to the basilica are a sun trap: grab a juice to take away from Shake Café (p57) and a bespoke *panino* from Mariano (p56).

A ☆15

Canale Macinante

Via Fosso Macinante

Viale Fratelli Rosselli

B

Via Montebello

Porta al Prato

C

Via il Prato

D

1

◉5
Parco delle Cascine

2

✕ Corso Italia
8

Via Magenta

Via G Garibaldi

Via Montebello

Via Palestro

Via Curtatone

Corso Italia

Lungarno Amerigo Vespucci

3

Arno

Lungarno di Santa Rosa

Ponte Amerigo Vespucci

4

Via dell'Anconella

Via Lungo le Mura di Santa Rosa

Via L Bartolini

Via Sant' Onofrio

Via del Piaggione

Via Pisana

For reviews see	
◉ Top Sights	p50
◉ Sights	p54
✕ Eating	p56
🍷 Drinking	p57
☆ Entertainment	p58
🛍 Shopping	p58

Viale Lodovico Ariosto

Piazza di Verzaia

Piazza dei Nerli

Piazza del Tiratoio

SAN FREDIANO

5

Ⓝ 0 ———— 200 m
0 ———— 0.1 miles

E

F

G

H

1

Via Luigi Alamanni

Via Valfonda

Via Fiume

Via Faenza

Largo Fratelli Alinari

Stazione di Santa Maria Novella

Piazza della Stazione

Via degli Orti Oricellari

Via della Scala

Via Santa Caterina da Siena

Via de' Panzani

Via Sant'Antonino

2

Piazza dell'Unità Italiana

Via Palazzuolo

Via dell'Albero

Basilica di Santa Maria Novella ⊙

Cappellone degli Spagnoli

Via de' Panzani

Via degli Avelli

⊙12

Via de' Canacci

Via de' Benedetta

🅐18

23🅐

Via Maso Finiguerra

⊗9

Via della Scala

Piazza di Santa Maria Novella

3

14

Via Meleghiano

Borgo d'Ognissanti

Piazza di San Paolino

Museo Novecento ⊙1

Via de' Fossi

19🅐 Via del Trabbio

Via degli Antinori

Chiesa d'Ognissanti ⊙4

Via del Porcellana

⊙2

Via della Spada

Via delle Belle Donne

Via de' Giacomini

Piazza d'Ognissanti

Piazza degli Ottaviani

17🅐

10

⊙13

Piazza San Pancrazio

Museo 7⊗

🅐20

4

11⊙

Via dei Fossi

Via del Moro

Via dei Palchetti

Museo Marino Marini

Via della Vigna Nuova

Via del Purgatorio

Via de' Tornabuoni

Piazza Carlo Goldoni

🅐16

22🅐 21🅐

Via del Parione

Via dell'Inferno

6⊗

Piazza di Cestello

Lungarno Soderini

Ponte alla Carraia

Lungarno Corsini

Via Parioncino

3⊙

Chiesa di Santa Trinita

Piazza Santa Trinita

5

Borgo San Frediano

Arno

Sights

Museo Novecento
MUSEUM

1 Map p52, G3

Don't allow the Renaissance to distract from Florence's fantastic modern art museum, in a 13th-century *palazzo* (mansion) previously used as a pilgrim shelter, hospital and school. A well-articulated itinerary guides visitors through modern Italian painting and sculpture from the early 20th century to the late 1980s. Installation art makes effective use of the outside space on the 1st-floor loggia. Fashion and theatre get a nod on the 2nd floor, and the itinerary ends with a 20-minute cinematic montage of the best films set in Florence. (Museum of the 20th Century; ☑055 28 61 32; www. museonovecento.it; Piazza di Santa Maria Novella 10; adult/reduced €8.50/4; ☺9am-7pm Mon-Wed, Sat & Sun, to 2pm Thu, to 11pm Fri summer, 9am-6pm Fri-Wed, to 2pm Thu winter)

Museo Marino Marini
GALLERY

2 Map p52, H4

Deconsecrated in the 19th century, Chiesa di San Pancrazio is home to this small art museum displaying sculptures, portraits and drawings by Pistoia-born sculptor Marino Marini (1901–80). But the highlight is the **Cappella Rucellai** with a tiny scale copy of Christ's Holy Sepulchre in Jerusalem – a Renaissance gem by Leon

Parco delle Cascine

Battista Alberti. The chapel was built between 1458 and 1467 for the tomb of wealthy Florentine banker and wool merchant Giovanni Rucellai. (☎055 21 94 32; http://museomarinomarini.it/; Piazza San Pancrazio 1; adult/reduced €6/4; ⏱10am-7pm Sat-Mon, to 1pm Wed-Fri)

Chiesa di Santa Trìnita CHURCH

3 Map p52, H5

Built in Gothic style and later given a mannerist facade, this 14th-century church shelters some of the city's finest frescoes: Lorenzo Monaco's *Annunciation* (1422) in **Cappella Bartholini Salimbeni** and eye-catching frescoes by Ghirlandaio depicting the life of St Francis of Assisi in **Cappella Sassetti**, right of the altar. The frescoes were painted between 1483 and 1485 and feature portraits of illustrious Florentines of the time; pop a €0.50 coin in the slot to illuminate the frescoes for two minutes. (Piazza Santa Trinita; ⏱8am-noon & 4-5.45pm Mon-Sat, 8-10.45am & 4-5.45pm Sun)

Chiesa d'Ognissanti CHURCH

4 Map p52, F4

Stroll along Borgo d'Ognissanti, from Piazza Carlo Goldoni towards ancient city gate Porta al Prato, past antiques shops and designer boutiques to reach this 13th-century church, built as part of a Benedictine monastery. Its highlight is Domenico Ghirlandaio's fresco of the *Madonna della Misericordia* protecting members of the Vespucci family, the church's main patrons. Amerigo

Street Art

Take a break from Renaissance art at **Street Levels Gallery** (☎339 2203607, 347 3387760; www.facebook.com/pg/StreetLevelsGalleriaFirenze; Via Palazzuolo 74r; ⏱10am-1pm & 3-7pm), a pioneering urban street-art gallery showcasing the work of local street artists. These include street-sign hacker Clet (p110); the stencil art of Hogre; and ExitEnter whose work is easily recognisable by the red balloons holding up the matchstick figures he draws. A highlight is the enigmatic Blub, whose caricatures of historical figures wearing goggles and diving masks adorn many a city wall – his art is known as *L'Arte Sa Nuotare* (Art Knows how to Swim). Check the gallery's Facebook page for workshops, cultural events, *aperitivi* (evening drinks) and other uber-cool happenings.

Vespucci, the Florentine navigator who gave his name to the American continent, is supposed to be the young boy whose head peeks between the Madonna and the old man. (☎055 239 87 00; Borgo d'Ognissanti 42; admission free; ⏱9am-12.30pm & 4-6pm Mon-Sat, 9-10am & 4-5.30pm Sun)

Parco delle Cascine PARK

5 Map p52, A1

Florence's largest park is dotted with playgrounds and is a great place to let the little 'uns loose. Families take over

Top Tip

Botticelli Essential

Having exhausted the master-pieces in the Uffizi Gallery, there is another essential stop for Botticelli aficionados: the early Renaissance artist's grave inside Chiesa d'Ognissanti (p55). The artist had requested to be buried at the feet of Simonetta Vespucci, the married woman whom Botticelli was said to be in love with and who served as a model for one of his greatest masterpieces, *Primavera* (*Spring*). Look for the simple round tombstone marked 'Sandro Filipepe' in the south transept. Botticelli grew up in a house on the same street and a pensive St Augustine, painted by him in 1480, hangs in the church.

at weekends and the park is a colourful scene with rollerbladers, kite-flyers, joggers and kids on bikes. In summer you can also use Le Pavoniere swimming pool. (Viale degli Olmi)

Eating

Mariano   SANDWICHES €

 6 Map p52, H5

Our favourite for its simplicity, around since 1973. From sunrise to sunset, this brick-vaulted, 13th-century cellar gently buzzes with Florentines propped at the counter sipping coffee or wine or eating salads and *panini*.

Come here for a coffee-and-pastry breakfast, light lunch, an *aperitivo* with cheese or salami tasting platter (€12), or a *panino* to eat on the move. (☑ 055 21 40 67; Via del Parione 19r; panini €3.50; ⊘ 8am-3pm & 5-7.30pm Mon-Fri, 8am-3pm Sat)

Trattoria Marione   TRATTORIA €€

 7 Map p52, H4

For the quintessential 'Italian dining' experience, Marione is gold. It's busy, it's noisy, it's 99.9% local and the cuisine is right out of Nonna's Tuscan kitchen. No one appears to speak English so go for Italian – the tasty excellent-value traditional fare is worth it. If you don't get a complimentary *limoncello* (lemon liqueur) with the bill, you clearly failed the language test. (☑ 055 21 47 56; Via della Spada 27; meals €30; ⊘ noon-3pm & 7-11pm)

Borderline   TUSCAN €€

 8 Map p52, B2

From the team behind the iconic Antica Trattoria Da Tito (around since 1913 in San Marco), Borderline is a stylish advocate of Tuscan culinary tradition. Inside an old theatre, it serves classic artichokes and wild boar pasta, and more creative fish dishes like seafood *ribollita* (Tuscan bread soup) and *orecchiette* (a type of pasta) with octopus sauce, to a staunchly local crowd. (☑ 055 28 87 71; www.borderline-firenze.com; Corso Italia 35; meals €35; ⊘ noon-3pm & 7.30pm-midnight)

Il Contadino
TRATTORIA €

9 Map p52, F3

Come the weekend, this no-frills trattoria gets packed with families lunching with gusto on its astonishingly good-value Tuscan cuisine. Lunch, moreover, is served until 3.30pm when the dinner menu kicks in, meaning convenient all-day dining. The day's menu includes 10 or so dishes, including meaty classics like roast rabbit, tripe and oven-roasted pork shank. Two-course lunch/dinner menus start at €9/13.50. (📞055 238 26 73; www.trattoriailcontadino.com; Via Palazzuolo 69-71r; meals €11-15; ⏰noon-10.30pm)

Drinking

Caffè Giacosa
CAFE

10 Map p52, H4

This chic cafe with 1815 pedigree was the inventor of the Negroni cocktail and hub of Anglo-Florentine sophistication during the interwar years. Today it is the hip cafe of local hotshot designer Roberto Cavalli, whose flagship boutique is next door. Giacosa is known for its refreshingly unelevated prices, excellent coffee and buzzing street terrace on fashionable Via de' Tornabuoni. (📞055 277 63 28; www.caffegiacosa.it; Via della Spada 10r; ⏰7.45am-8.30pm Mon-Fri, 8.30am-8.30pm Sat, 12.30-8.30pm Sun; 📶)

Local Life
Cheap Romance

Before sunset, follow the lead of savvy, budget-conscious Florentines: buy a bottle of wine and head to the hottest seats in town – the smooth, stone platform created by the east-facing bridge supports of **Ponte Santa Trìnita**. Sit above the swirling water and toast the sun as it sinks behind the romantic, star-lit Ponte Vecchio further down the river.

Todo Modo
CAFE

11 Map p52, G4

This contemporary bookshop with hip cafe and pocket theatre at the back makes a refreshing change from the usual offerings. A salvaged mix of vintage tables and chairs sits between book- and bottle-lined shelves in the relaxed cafe, actually called 'UqBar' after the fictional place of the same name in a short story by Argentinian writer Jorges Luis Borges. (📞055 239 91 10; www.todomodo.org; Via dei Fossi 15r; ⏰10am-8pm Tue-Sun)

Shake Café
CAFE

12 Map p52, H3

Handily close to the train station, this self-service juice bar has a perfect people-watching pavement terrace on car-free Piazza di Santa Maria Novella. Its fruit-powered juices and smoothies

Top Tip

What the Locals Drink...

Go local in summer with a cooling Caffè de' Medici, aka a cold shaken espresso topped with whipped cream, chocolate and hazelnuts. Caffè Giacosa (p57) is the hot spot to try it.

include fabulous combos such as pineapple, fennel, celery, mint, chicory and liquorice. Unusually for Florence, Shake Café also makes cappuccinos with soy, almond or rice milk. Salads, wraps, sandwiches and gelato stave off hunger pangs. (☑055 29 53 10; www.shakecafe.bio; Via degli Avelli 2r; ⏱7am-8pm)

Sei Divino   WINE BAR

 13   Map p52, F4

This stylish wine bar tucked beneath a red-brick vaulted ceiling is a veteran on Florence's prolific wine-bar scene. Come here for music and occasional exhibitions as well as fine wine. *Aperitivi* 'hour' (with copious banquet) runs from 7pm to 10pm, with a buoyant crowd spilling outside onto the pavement in summer. (☑055 21 57 94; Borgo d'Ognissanti 42r; ⏱6pm-1am Wed-Mon)

Space Club   CLUB

 14   Map p52, F3

Sheer size alone at this vast nightclub in Santa Maria Novella impresses – dancing, drinking, video-karaoke in the bar, and a mixed student-international crowd. (☑055 29 30 82;

www.facebook.com/spacefirenze2; Via Palazzuolo 37r; admission variable; ⏱10pm-4am)

Entertainment

Opera di Firenze   OPERA

 15   Map p52, A1

Florence's strikingly modern opera house with glittering contemporary geometric facade sits on the green edge of city park Parco delle Cascine. Its three thoughtfully designed and multifunctional concert halls seat an audience of 5000 and play host to the springtime **Maggio Musicale Fiorentino**. (☑055 277 93 09; www.operadifirenze.it; Piazzale Vittorio Gui, Viale Fratelli Rosselli 15; ⏱box office 10am-6pm Tue-Fri, to 1pm Sat)

Shopping

Benheart   FASHION & ACCESSORIES

 16   Map p52, G4

Evocative of an artisan workshop, this tiny boutique showcases the world-class leather craft of local superstar Benheart. The young Florentine fashion designer went into business with Florentine schoolmate Matteo after undergoing a heart transplant. The pair swore that if Ben survived, they would set up shop on their own. Their handmade shoes (from €250), for men and women, are among the finest in Florence. (☑055 239 94 83; www.benheart.it; Via della Vigna Nuova 97r; ⏱9am-8pm Mon-Sat, 10am-8pm Sun)

Mio Concept

HOMEWARES

17 🔒 Map p52, H4

A fascinating range of design objects for the home – many upcycled – as well as jewellery, T-shirts and street art cram this stylish boutique created by German-born globetrotter Antje. This is also the only shop in town to sell street-sign artworks by Florence-based street artist Clet (p110); limited edition street signs, of which Clet produces just 13 of each design, start at €2500. (☑ 055 264 55 43; www.mio-concept.com; Via della Spada 34r; ◷10am-1.30pm & 2.30-7.30pm Tue-Sat, 3-7pm Mon)

Officina Profumo-Farmaceutica di Santa Maria Novella

BEAUTY, GIFTS

18 🔒 Map p52, G3

In business since 1612, this exquisite perfumery-pharmacy began life when Santa Maria Novella's Dominican friars began to concoct cures and sweet-smelling unguents using medicinal herbs cultivated in the monastery garden. The shop, with an interior from 1848, sells fragrances, skincare products, ancient herbal remedies and preparations for everything from relief of heavy legs to improving skin elasticity, memory and mental energy. (☑ 055 21 62 76; www.smnovella.it; Via della Scala 16; ◷9.30am-8pm)

🔍 Local Life

Picnic Perfect

Follow the trail of knowing Florentines, past the flower- and veg-laden bicycle parked outside, into **La Bottega Della Frutta** (☑ 055 239 85 90; Via dei Federighi 31r; ◷8.30am-7.30pm Mon-Sat, closed Aug), an enticing food shop bursting with boutique cheeses, organic fruit and veg, biscuits, chocolates, conserved produce, excellent-value wine et al. Mozzarella oozing raw milk arrives fresh from Eboli in Sicily every Tuesday, and if you're looking to buy olive oil, this is the place to taste. Simply ask Elisabeta or her husband, Francesco.

Aprosio & Co

ACCESSORIES, JEWELLERY

19 🔒 Map p52, H3

Ornella Aprosio fashions teeny-tiny glass and crystal beads into dazzling pieces of jewellery, hair accessories, animal-shaped brooches, handbags, even glass-flecked cashmere. It is all quite magical. (☑ 055 21 01 27; www.aprosio.it; Via del Moro 75-77r; ◷10am-7pm Mon-Fri, 10.30am-7.30pm Sat)

Grevi

FASHION & ACCESSORIES

20 🔒 Map p52, H4

It was a hat made by Siena milliner Grevi that actress Cher wore in the film *Tea with Mussolini* (1999); ditto

Local Life
Trainspotting

Most people rush through Florence's main train station, **Stazione di Santa Maria Novella** (Map p52, 1G) Piazza della Stazione), without a second glance, but in fact it's one of Italy's great modernist buildings. Built in the early 1930s, the station's plain facade mimics the rough stone of churches such as San Lorenzo, while the red-and-white striped marble floors recall the city's official colours.

Maggie Smith in *My House in Umbria* (2003). So if you want to shop like a star for a hat by Grevi, this hopelessly romantic boutique is the address. Hats range in price from €30 to possibly unaffordable. (✆055 26 41 39; www.grevi.it; Via della Spada 11-13r; ⏱10am-2pm & 3-8pm Mon-Sat)

Pineider ARTS & CRAFTS

21 Map p52, H4

Stendhal, Byron, Shelley and Dickens are among the literary luminaries who have chosen to purchase top-quality stationery from this company. (✆055 28 46 56; www.pineider.com; Piazza de' Rucellai 4-7r; ⏱10am-7pm)

Letizia Fiorini ARTS & CRAFTS

22 Map p52, G5

This charming shop is a one-woman affair – Letizia Fiorini sits at the counter and makes her distinctive puppets by hand in between assisting customers. You'll find Pulchinella (Punch), Arlecchino the clown, beautiful servant girl Colombina, Doctor Peste (complete with plague mask), cheeky Brighella, swashbuckling Il Capitano and many other characters from traditional Italian puppetry. (✆055 21 65 04; Via del Parione 60r; ⏱10am-7pm Tue-Sat)

Dolceforte CHOCOLATE

23 Map p52, F3

Elena is the passion and knowledge behind this astonishing chocolate shop that sells only the best. Think black-truffle-flavoured chocolate, an entire cherry, stone and all, soaked in grappa and wrapped in white chocolate or – for the ultimate taste sensation – *formaggio di fossa* (a cheese from central Italy) soaked in sweet wine and enrobed in dark chocolate. (✆055 21 91 16; www.dolceforte.it; Via della Scala 21; ⏱10am-1pm & 3.30-7.45pm Wed-Sat & Mon, 3.30-7.45pm Tue)

Understand

The Renaissance

Though its streets and buildings date predominantly to the Middle Ages, it is the historical period known as the Renaissance (Rinascimento, or Rebirth) that defines Florence and remains its greatest moment.

In the second half of the 14th century, the city's powerbrokers were keen to put the horrors of the plague of 1348, when more than 50% of the city's residents had perished, behind them. This catastrophic event had dealt a huge blow to their faith in God – what was truly powerful, they reasoned, was the intellect, resilience and beauty of human beings. The Renaissance preoccupation with Humanism was born.

An early and passionate convert to this way of thinking was Cosimo de' Medici (1389–1464), who used his massive fortune to fund a program of inspired cultural patronage. Painters, sculptors and architects were lured to Florence by the financial incentives and artistic opportunities he offered. Often inspired by the culture of classical antiquity, their works were as likely to celebrate the human body (eg Michelangelo's *David*)or a pagan myth (Botticelli's *Birth of Venus*) as they were to rework a standard religious theme. In architecture, the classical inspiration was even more pronounced, with Brunelleschi's design for the cathedral's massive dome forming the gold standard.

Alongside these developments in art and architecture was the flowering of Italian literature. Dante Alghieri's *La grande commedia* (The Great Comedy, later renamed the Divine Comedy) had been published around 1317 and established the Tuscan dialect as the new standardised form of written Italian. Giovanni Boccaccio (1303–75) and Francesco Petrarch (1304–74) were quick adopters.

In the 15th and 16th centuries, developments in art, architecture and literature were matched by those in philosophy, political science and science, and Florence became home to a formidable intellectual milieu. This included artist, architect, scientist, engineer and all-round 'Renaissance man', Leonardo da Vinci (1452–1519); and writer, historian and political scientist, Niccolò Machiavelli (1469–1527).

As the 16th century drew to a close, so too did the Italian Renaissance. Fortunately, its heritage lives on and is showcased in the city's cultural institutions and deep appreciation (some would say obsession) with all things artistic.

Explore

San Lorenzo & San Marco

This part of the city fuses a gutsy market precinct – covered produce market and noisy street stalls surrounding the Basilica di San Lorenzo – with capacious Piazza San Marco, home to Florence University and a much-loved monastery museum. Between the two is the world's most famous sculpture, *David*. The result is a sensory experience jam-packed with urban grit and uplifting art.

The Sights in a Day

☼ Open the day with serious coffee at **Ditta Al Cinema** (p74). Walk to the **Mercato Centrale** (p71): there is no more vibrant part of the city to really lap up local life at its gritty, day-to-day best than this covered food market, abuzz with energy. Mooch its food stall, taste and buy Tuscan olive oil, then head to your next ports of call: **Basilica di San Lorenzo** (p68), **Biblioteca Medicea Laurenziana** (p68) and **Museo delle Cappelle Medicee** (p68); the latter two open mornings only.

☼ Medici opulence appreciated, head into San Marco where the **Museo di San Marco** (p69) rewards with Fra' Angelico's haunting frescoes – the museum closes at 1.50pm. Grab a light bite at **Pugi** (p74) or late lunch with fashionable Florentines at **La Ménagère** (p71).

☾ Spend a slower-paced afternoon in the **Galleria dell'Accademia** (p64), admiring the bewitching, concentrated expression of Michelangelo's *David*. Cool off afterwards with a gelato from the hottest gelateria of the moment, artisanal **My Sugar** (p72). Devote the evening to Tuscan cuisine at **Antica Trattoria da Tito** (p73) and craft cocktails at **Lo Sverso** (p73).

 Top Sight

Galleria dell'Accademia (p64)

♥ **Best of Florence**

Eating
Trattoria Mario (p71)

Trattoria Sergio Gozzi (p72)

La Ménagère (p71)

My Sugar (p72)

Drinking
Lo Sverso (p73)

Shopping
Mercato Centrale (p71)

Street Doing (p75)

Scriptorium (p75)

Penko (p76)

Getting There

⏱ **Walk** From Piazza della Stazione walk southeast along Via de' Panzani and turn left (northeast) into Via del Giglio, which takes you to the Museo dell Cappelle Medicee, Piazza San Lorenzo and Basilica di San Lorenzo. Then walk east along Via de' Pucci and north into Via Ricasoli to reach the Galleria dell'Accademia and Piazza San Marco.

Top Sights
Galleria dell'Accademia

A lengthy queue marks the door to this gallery, purpose-built to house one of the Renaissance's greatest masterpieces, Michelangelo's *David*. Fortunately, the world's most famous statue is worth the wait. Also here are Michelangelo's unfinished *Prigioni* sculpture and paintings by Andrea Orcagna, Taddeo Gaddi, Domenico Ghirlandaio, Filippino Lippi and Sandro Botticelli.

◉ Map p66, E3

www.firenzemusei.it

Via Ricasoli 60

adult/reduced €8/4, incl temporary exhibition €12.50/6.25

🕗 8.15am-6.50pm Tue-Sun

Coronazione della Vergine, by Jacopo Cambi

Michelangelo's David

Carved from a single block of marble already worked on by two sculptors, Michelangelo's most famous work was challenging to complete. Yet the subtle detail of the enormous work of art – the veins in his sinewy arms, the leg muscles, the change in expression as you move around the statue – is indeed impressive. Thankfully for Michelangelo, when the statue of the nude boy-warrior – depicted for the first time as a man rather than young boy – appeared on Piazza della Signoria in 1504, Florentines immediately adopted *David* as an emblem of power, liberty and civic pride.

The Slaves

Another soul-soaring work by Michelangelo, *Prigioni* (1521–30) evokes four 'prisoners' or 'slaves' so powerfully that the figures really do seem to be writhing and struggling to free themselves from the ice-cold marble. The work was intended for the tomb of Pope Julius II in Rome, which was never completed.

Coronation of the Virgin

This remarkable piece of embroidery – an altar frontal 4m long and over 1m wide – portrays the *Coronazione della Vergine* (*Coronation of the Virgin;* 1336) in exquisite detail using polychrome silks and gold and silver thread. Completed by master embroiderer Jacopo Cambi, it originally covered the high altar of the Basilica di Santa Maria Novella.

Botticelli's Madonna

Madonna del Mare (*Madonna of the Sea;* 1477), a portrait of the Virgin and child by Sandro Botticelli, exudes a mesmerising serenity. Compare it with works in the gallery by Botticelli's master and mentor, Filippo Lippi (c 1457–1504), to whom some critics attribute it.

☑ **Top Tips**

▶ Book tickets in advance at Firenze Musei (p182): the reservation fee is €4.

▶ Trail the world's best-known naked man around town: admire *David* copies on Piazza della Signoria and Piazzale Michelangelo; see Davids sculpted by other artists in Museo del Bargello.

▶ Visit on the first Sunday of the month when admission is free.

✘ **Take a Break**

Keep cool in the queue with a gelato or almond *granita* (ice drink) from Sicilian-style ice-cream shop, Carabé (p73).

Grab a quick bite from Pugi (p74) bakery, a favourite for pizza slices and *schiacciata* (Tuscan flatbread), spiked with salt and rosemary.

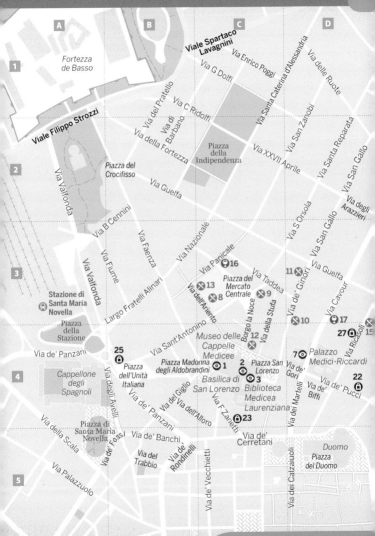

Fortezza
de Basso

A
B
C
D

Viale Spartaco
Lavagnini

Via G Dolfi

Via Enrico Poggi

Viale Filippo Strozzi

Via del Pratello

Via C Ridolfi

Via di Barbano

Via della Fortezza

Piazza del
Crocifisso

Piazza
della
Indipendenza

Via Santa Caterina d'Alessandria

Via delle Ruote

Via San Zanobi

Via Santa Reparata

Via San Gallo

Via XXVII Aprile

Via Guelfa

Via Valfonda

Via B Cennini

Via Faenza

Via Nazionale

Via S Orsola

Via San Gallo

Via degli Arazzieri

Via Flume

Via Valfonda

Largo Fratelli Alinari

Stazione di
Santa Maria
Novella

Piazza
della
Stazione

Via de' Panzani

Cappellone
degli
Spagnoli

Piazza di
Santa Maria
Novella

Via della Scala

Via Palazzuolo

Via de' Fossi

Via degli Avelli

Via Sant'Antonino

Via Panicale

Via dell'Ariento

Via del Giglio

Via de' Panzani

Via de' Banchi

Via del Trabbio

Via de' Rondinelli

Via de' Vecchietti

Via de' Va dell'Alloro

Via F Zanetti

Via de' Cerretani

Borgo la Noce

Via della Stufa

Via Taddea

Piazza del
Mercato
Centrale

Museo delle
Cappelle
Medicee

Piazza Madonna
degli Aldobrandini

Piazza San
Lorenzo

Basilica di
San Lorenzo

Biblioteca
Medicea
Laurenziana

Via de' Gori

Via de' Martelli

Via de' Calzaiuoli

Via de' Ginori

Via Guelfa

Via Cavour

Via Ricasoli

Palazzo
Medici-Riccardi

Via de' Pucci

Via de' Biffi

Duomo

Piazza
del Duomo

16
13
8
9
11
10
17
27
15
12
25
1
2
3
23
7
22

1
2
3
4
5

Via Zara

Via San Gallo

Via Cavour

Via Alfonso Lamarmora

Via Venezia

Via Gustavo Modena

Viale Giacomo Matteotti

Piazza I del Lungo

✗ 14

Via Pier Antonio Micheli

Via Gino Capponi

Via Giorgio La Pira

Giardino dei Semplici

Giardino della Gherardesca

Piazzale Donatello

Museo di San Marco
4 👁

Piazza San Marco

Via Ricasoli

Via Cesare Battisti

Chiesa della Santissima Annunziata
👁 6

Via Giuseppe Giusti

Borgo Pinti

Cimitero degli Inglesi

👁 **Galleria dell'Accademia**

Piazza della SS Annunziata

Via della Fibbiai

👁 5
Museo degli Innocenti

Via Laura

Via della Colonna

Via Vittorio Alfieri

21 🔒
26 🔒

Via dei Servi

Via del Castellaccio

Piazza Brunelleschi

Via degli Alfani

Borgo Pinti

Piazza Massimo d'Azeglio

Via Bufalini

20 ✪

Via della Pergola

Via Nuova de' Caccini

Via dei Pilastri

Via Luigi Carlo Farini

Via Giosuè Carducci

Piazza di Santa Maria Nuova

Via Sant'Egidio

Borgo Pinti

18 🍷
Via Fiesolana

Via de' Pepi

Via della Mattonaia

Via dell'Oriuolo

🔒 24

Via di Mezzo

🍷 19

200 m
0.1 miles

Sights

Museo delle Cappelle Medicee
MAUSOLEUM

1 Map p66, C4

Nowhere is Medici conceit expressed so explicitly as in the Medici Chapels. Adorned with granite, marble, semi-precious stones and some of Michelangelo's most beautiful sculptures, it is the burial place of 49 dynasty members. Francesco I lies in the dark, imposing **Cappella dei Principi** (Princes' Chapel) alongside Ferdinando I and II and Cosimo I, II and III. Lorenzo il Magnifico is buried in the graceful **Sagrestia Nuova** (New Sacristy), which was Michelangelo's first architectural work. (Medici

---

Top Tip

Michelangelo Essential

For hardcore Michelangelo lovers, no sculptures are more haunting or serenely beautiful than those decorating Medici graves in the sacristy of the Museo delle Cappelle Medicee: *Dawn and Dusk* on the sarcophagus of Lorenzo, Duke of Urbino; *Night and Day* on the sarcophagus of Lorenzo's son Giuliano (note the unfinished face of 'Day' and the youth of the sleeping woman drenched in light aka 'Night'); and *Madonna and Child,* which adorns Lorenzo's tomb.

Chapels; www.firenzemusei.it; Piazza Madonna degli Aldobrandini 6; adult/reduced €8/4; ⏰8.15am-1.50pm, closed 1st, 3rd & 5th Mon, 2nd & 4th Sun of month)

Basilica di San Lorenzo
BASILICA

2 Map p66, C4

Considered one of Florence's most harmonious examples of Renaissance architecture, this unfinished basilica was the Medici parish church and mausoleum. It was designed by Brunelleschi in 1425 for Cosimo the Elder and built over a 4th-century church. In the solemn interior, look for Brunelleschi's austerely beautiful **Sagrestia Vecchia** (Old Sacristy) with its sculptural decoration by Donatello. Michelangelo was commissioned to design the facade in 1518, but his design in white Carrara marble was never executed, hence the building's rough, unfinished appearance. (www.operamedicealaurenziana.org; Piazza San Lorenzo; €6, with Biblioteca Medicea Laurenziana €8.50; ⏰10am-5pm Mon-Sat, plus 1.30-5pm Sun Mar-Oct)

Biblioteca Medicea Laurenziana
LIBRARY

3 Map p66, C4

Beyond the Basilica di San Lorenzo ticket office lie peaceful cloisters framing a garden with orange trees. Stairs lead up the loggia to the Biblioteca Medicea Laurenziana**,** commissioned by Giulio de' Medici (Pope Clement

VII) in 1524 to house the extensive Medici library (started by Cosimo the Elder and greatly added to by Lorenzo il Magnifico). The extraordinary staircase in the vestibule, intended as a 'dark prelude' to the magnificent **Sala di Lettura** (Reading Room), was designed by Michelangelo. (Medici Library; ☎ 055 293 79 11; www.bml.firenze. sbn.it; Piazza San Lorenzo 9; €3, incl basilica €8.50; ☺ 9.30am-1.30pm Mon-Sat)

Museo di San Marco   MUSEUM

4 ◎ Map p66, E2

At the heart of Florence's university area sits **Chiesa di San Marco** and an adjoining 15th-century Dominican monastery where both gifted painter Fra' Angelico (c 1395–1455) and the sharp-tongued Savonarola piously served God. Today the monastery, aka one of Florence's most spiritually uplifting museums, showcases the work of Fra' Angelico. After centuries of being known as 'Il Beato Angelico' (literally 'The Blessed Angelic One') or simply 'Il Beato' (The Blessed), the Renaissance's most blessed religious painter was made a saint by Pope John Paul II in 1984. (☎ 055 238 86 08; Piazza San Marco 3; adult/reduced €4/2; ☺ 8.15am-1.50pm Mon-Fri, 8.15am-4.50pm Sat & Sun, closed 1st, 3rd & 5th Sun, 2nd & 4th Mon of month)

Basilica di San Lorenzo

Museo degli Innocenti   MUSEUM

5 Map p66, F3

Shortly after its founding in 1421, Brunelleschi designed the loggia for Florence's **Ospedale degli Innocenti**, a foundling hospital and Europe's first orphanage, built by the wealthy silk weavers' guild to care for unwanted children. Inside, a highly emotive, state-of-the-art museum explores its history, climaxing with a sensational collection of frescoes and artworks that once decorated the hospital and a stunning rooftop cafe terrace (fab city views). Brunelleschi's use of rounded arches and Roman capitals mark it as arguably the first building of the Renaissance. (☎055 203 73 08; www. museodeglinnocenti.it; Piazza della Santissima Annunziata 13; adult/reduced/family €7/5/10; ☺10am-7pm)

Chiesa della Santissima Annunziata   CHURCH

6 Map p66, F3

Established in 1250 by the founders of the Servite order and rebuilt by Michelozzo and others in the mid-15th-century, this Renaissance church is most remarkable for the post-Renaissance painters who worked here together and helped found the mannerist school. There are frescoes by Andrea del Castagno in the first two chapels on the left of the church, and the frescoes in Michelozzo's atrium include work by del Sarto as well as Jacopo Pontormo and Il Rosso Fiorentino (the Redhead

from Florence). (Piazza della Santissima Annunziata; ☺7.30am-12.30pm & 4-6.30pm)

Palazzo Medici-Riccardi   PALACE

7 Map p66, D4

Cosimo the Elder entrusted Michelozzo with the design of the family's townhouse in 1444. The result was this palace, a blueprint that influenced the construction of Florentine family residences such as Palazzo Pitti and Palazzo Strozzi. The upstairs chapel, **Cappella dei Magi**, is covered in wonderfully detailed frescoes (c 1459–63) by Benozzo Gozzoli, a pupil of Fra' Angelico, and is one of the supreme achievements of Renaissance painting. (☎055 276 03 40; www.

✓ Top Tip

Visiting Cappella dei Magi

Only 10 visitors are allowed at a time into the Cappella dei Magi, squirrelled away inside Palazzo Medici-Riccardi. In high season, reserve in advance at the ticket desk. During your visit, take time to spy various Medici family members in Gozzoli's frescoes, whose ostensible theme of Procession of the Magi to Bethlehem is but a slender pretext for portraying members of the Medici clan in their best light; spy Lorenzo il Magnifico and Cosimo the Elder in the crowd. Should you be wondering, the chapel was reconfigured to accommodate a baroque staircase, hence the oddly split fresco.

palazzo-medici.it; Via Cavour 3; adult/reduced €7/4; ⊘8.30am-7pm Thu-Tue)

Eating

Mercato Centrale

FOOD HALL €

8 Map p66, C3

Wander the maze of stalls rammed with fresh produce at Florence's oldest and largest food market, on the ground floor of a fantastic iron-and-glass structure designed by architect Giuseppe Mengoni in 1874. Head to the 1st floor's buzzing, thoroughly contemporary food hall with dedicated bookshop, cookery school and artisan stalls cooking steaks, burgers, tripe *panini,* vegetarian dishes, pizza, gelato, pastries and pasta. (☑055 239 97 98; www.mercatocentrale.it; Piazza del Mercato Centrale 4; dishes €7-15; ⊘10am-midnight; 🛜)

Trattoria Mario

TUSCAN €

9 Map p66, C3

Arrive by noon to ensure a stool around a shared table at this noisy, busy, brilliant trattoria – a legend that retains its soul (and allure with locals) despite being in every guidebook. Charming Fabio, whose grandfather opened the place in 1953, is front of house while big brother Romeo and nephew Francesco cook with speed in the kitchen. No advance reservations, no credit cards. (☑055 21 85 50; www.trattoria-mario.com; Via Rosina 2; meals €25; ⊘noon-3.30pm Mon-Sat, closed 3 weeks Aug; ❄)

La Ménagère

INTERNATIONAL €€

10 Map p66, D3

Be it breakfast, lunch, dinner, good coffee or cocktails after dark, this bright industrial-styled space lures Florence's hip brigade. A concept store, the Housewife is a fashionable one-stop shop for chic china and tableware, designer kitchen gear and fresh flowers. For daytime dining and drinking, pick from retro sofas in the boutique area, or banquette seating and bar stools in the jam-packed bistro. (☑055 075 06 00; www.lamenagere. it; Via de' Ginori 8r; meals €15-70; ⊘7am-2am; 🛜)

Top Tip

Florence's Finest Last Supper

Once part of a sprawling Benedictine monastery, the largely unsung **Cenacolo di Sant'Apollonia** (☑055 238 86 07; www.polomusealetoscana. beniculturali.it; Via XXVII Apre 1; admission free; ⏱8.15am-1.50pm daily, closed 1st, 3rd & 5th Sat & Sun of month) harbours arguably the city's most remarkable Last Supper scene. Painted by Andrea del Castagno in the 1440s, it is one of the first works of its kind to effectively apply Renaissance perspective. It possesses a haunting power with its vivid colours – especially the almost abstract squares of marble painted above the Apostles' heads – as well as the dark, menacing figure of Judas.

My Sugar   GELATO €

 11 Map p66, D3

Young artisan ice-cream maker, Alberto Bati, partner Giulia and sister Deborah have taken the city by storm with their thoroughly contemporary, artisan gelateria near Piazza San Marco. The 16 sensational flavours include dark chocolate with Chianti red wine, ginger mandarin, black sesame and Araminta (a wonderful palette-cleansing fusion of mint, orange and cinnamon). Frozen yoghurt and milkshakes too. Cash only. (☑393 0696042; Via de' Ginori 49r; cones €2-2.50, tubs €2-5; ⏱1-9pm)

Trattoria Sergio Gozzi   TRATTORIA €

 12 Map p66, C4

Keep things simple with a traditional Tuscan lunch at this two-room trattoria, tucked between cheap leather shops near Mercato Centrale. Dining is at marble-topped tables in a spartan vintage interior clearly unchanged since 1915 when it opened. Expect all the classics: plenty of pasta, roast meats, tripe and *bollito misto* (boiled beef, chicken and tongue) included. (☑055 28 19 41; Piazza San Lorenzo 8r; meals €25; ⏱10am-4pm Mon-Sat)

Da Nerbone   FAST FOOD €

 13 Map p66, C3

Forge your way past cheese, meat and sausage stalls on the ground floor of Florence's Mercato Centrale to join the lunchtime queue at Nerbone, in the biz since 1872. Go local and order *trippa alla fiorentina* (tripe and tomato stew) or follow the crowd with a feisty *panini con bollito* (a hefty

 Local Life

A Secret Terrace

When the crowds get too much, retreat to the elegant rooftop cafe of the Museo degli Innocenti (p70) for an *aperitivo* (early evening drink). There is no finer time to enjoy the sweeping panorama from this 'secret' terrace than at dusk when the sun turns the city pink.

Top Tip

Fish Friday, Steak Saturday

In the finest of Tuscan dining tradition, many atrattoria address in Florence cooks up a different traditional dish each day of the week. For the folks at Trattoria Mario (p71), Monday and Thursday are tripe days, Friday is fish and Saturday sees local Florentines flock in for a brilliantly blue *bisteca alla fiorentina* (traditonal Florentine T-bone steak).

boiled-beef bun, dunked in the meat's juices before serving). Eat standing up or fight for a table. (Mercato Centrale, Piazza del Mercato Centrale; meals €10; ⏱7am-2pm Mon-Sat)

Antica Trattoria da Tito   TRATTORIA €€

 14 ✗ Map p66, E1

The 'No well done meat here' sign, strung in the window, says it all: the best of Tuscan culinary tradition is the only thing this iconic trattoria serves. In business since 1913, Da Tito does everything right – tasty Tuscan dishes like onion soup and wild boar pasta, served with friendly gusto and hearty goodwill to a local crowd. Don't be shy to enter. (☎055 47 24 75; www.trattoria datito.it; Via San Gallo 112r; meals €30; ⏱noon-3pm & 7-11pm Mon-Sat)

Carabé   GELATO €

 15 ✗ Map p66, D4

Traditional Sicilian gelato, *granita* (crushed ice made with coffee, fresh fruit or locally grown pistachios and almonds) and brioche (Sicilian ice-cream sandwich); handy if you're waiting in line to see *David*. (☎055 28 94 76; www.parcocarabe.it; Via Ricasoli 60r; cones €2.50-4; ⏱10am-midnight, closed mid-Dec–mid-Jan)

Drinking

Lo Sverso   COCKTAIL BAR

 16 🍷 Map p66, C3

In a part of town where drinking holes are unusually scarce, stylish Lo Sverso is a real gem. Bartenders shake cocktails using homemade syrups (any cocktail using their feisty basil syrup is a winner), the craft beers – several on tap – are among the best in Florence and their home-brewed ginger ale is worth a visit in its own right. (☎335 5473530; www.facebook.com/losverso.firenze; Via Panicale 7-9r; ⏱5pm-1am Mon-Sat, to midnight Sun)

Q Local Life

Hipster Hang-out

Whatever the time of day, uber-cool concept store and bistro La Ménagère (p71) is the hot spot to hobnob with Florentine hipsters; this all-round hybrid is a great breakfast spot, too.

Top Tip

Pugi

Should you be queuing to see *David*, **Pugi** (Map p66, E3; 📞055 28 09 81; www.focacceria-pugi.it; Piazza San Marco 9b; per kg €15-24; ⏱7.45am-8pm Mon-Sat, closed 2 weeks mid-Aug) is a perfect two-minute hop from the Galleria dell'Accademia. The inevitable line outside the door says it all. The bakery is a Florentine favourite for pizza slices and chunks of *schiacciata* (Tuscan flatbread) baked up plain, spiked with salt and rosemary, or topped or stuffed with whatever delicious edible goodies are in season. Grab a numbered ticket, drool over the sweet and savoury treats demanding to be devoured, and wait for your number to be called.

Ditta Al Cinema
CAFE, BAR

17 Map p66, D3

At home in Florence's historic La Compagnia cinema, the third and most recent space of iconic coffee roaster and gin bar Ditta Artigianiale doesn't disappoint. Some 150 different labels of gin jostle for the limelight at the bar, while barman Lorenzo's cocktail list plays on the cinema's heritage with drinks named after movie classics. Breakfast, lunch, brunch and all-day tapas too. (📞055 045 71 63; Via Cavour 50r; ⏱8am-midnight Mon-Fri, 9am-midnight Sat & Sun; 🛜)

Rex Caffé
BAR

18 Map p66, F5

A firm long-term favourite since 1990, down-to-earth Rex maintains its appeal. Behind the bar Virginia and Lorenzo shake a mean cocktail, using homemade syrups and artisanal spirits like ginger- or carrot-flavoured vodka, pepper rum and laurel vermouth. The artsy, Gaudí-inspired interior is as much art gallery and nightlife stage as simple bar. DJ sets at weekends and bags of fun events. (📞055 248 03 31; www.rexfirenze.com; Via Fiesolana 25r; ⏱6pm-3am)

Chillax Lounge Bar
BAR

19 Map p66, F5

Kick back with a cocktail and chill in a predominantly wood interior at this lounge bar on the fringe of nightlife-hot Santa Croce. Music – both live and DJ sets – covers all sounds, including Latin, salsa, pop and rock. Wednesday is often karaoke night; check its Facebook page for events. (📞346 2656340; Via Fiesolana 8-10r; ⏱10pm-4am Tue-Sun)

Entertainment

Teatro della Pergola
THEATRE

20 ⭐ Map p66, F4

Beautiful city theatre with stunning entrance; host to classical concerts October to April. (📞055 2 26 41; www.teatrodellapergola.com; Via della Pergola 18)

 Da Nerbone (p72)

Shopping

Street Doing

FASHION, VINTAGE

 21 Map p66, E4

Vintage couture for men and women is what this extraordinary rabbit warren of a boutique – surely the city's largest collection of vintage – is about. Carefully curated garments and acessories are in excellent condition and feature all the top Italian designers: beaded 1950s Gucci clutch bags, floral 1960s Pucci dresses, Valentino shades from every decade. Fashionistas, *this* is heaven. (☏055 538 13 34; www.street doingvintage.it; Via dei Servi 88r; ⊙2.30-7.30pm Mon, 10.30am-7.30pm Tue-Sat)

Scriptorium

ARTS & CRAFTS

22 Map p66, D4

A mooch around this upmarket boutique is worth it, if only to dip into the utterly cinematic courtyard of 16th- to 18th-century Palazzo Pucci in which it's hidden. Scriptorium crafts exquisite leather boxes and books, calligraphy nibs and pens, and old-world wax seals in every colour under the sun. (☏055 238 26 20; www.facebook.com/scriptoriumatelier/; Via de' Pucci 4; ⊙10am-1pm & 3.30-7pm Mon-Fri, 10am-1pm Sat)

Penko
JEWELLERY

23 🔒 Map p66, C4

Renaissance jewels and gems inspire
the designs of third-generation jeweller Paolo Penko who works with his
son in the atelier his grandfather
opened in the 1950s. Everything is
handmade, as the mass of vintage
tools strewn on the workbench attests.
Drop in at the right moment and Paolo
can mint you your very own Florentine
florin in bronze, silver or gold. (📞055
21 16 61; www.paolopenko.com; Via Ferdinando
Zannetti 14-16r; ⏱9.30am-7pm Mon-Sat)

Mrs Macis
FASHION & ACCESSORIES

24 🔒 Map p66, F5

Workshop and showroom of the
talented Carla Macis, this eye-catching
boutique – dollhouse-like in design –
specialises in very feminine 1950s, '60s
and '70s clothes and jewellery made
from new and recycled fabrics. Every
piece is unique and fabulous. (📞055
247 67 00; Borgo Pinti 38r; ⏱4-7.30pm Mon,
10.30am-1pm & 4-7.30pm Tue-Sat)

A Florentine florin

Understand

Who's That Bloke?

Name *David*
Occupation World's most famous sculpture
Vital statistics Height: 516cm tall; weight: 19 tonnes of mediocre-quality pearly white marble from the Fantiscritti quarries in Carrara.
Spirit Young biblical hero in meditative pose who, with the help of God, defeats an enemy more powerful than himself. Scarcely visible sling emphasises victory of innocence and intellect over brute force.
Commissioned In 1501 by the Opera del Duomo for the cathedral, but subsequently placed in front of the Palazzo Vecchio on Piazza della Signoria, where it stayed until 1873.
Famous journeys It took 40 men four days to transport the statue on rails from Michelangelo's workshop behind the cathedral to Piazza della Signoria in 1504. Its journey from here, through the streets of Florence, to its current purpose-built tribune in the Galleria dell'Accademia in 1873 took seven long days.
Outstanding features (a) His expression which, from the left profile, appears serene, Zen and boylike, and from the right, concentrated, manly and highly charged in anticipation of the gargantuan Goliath he is about to slay; (b) the sense of counterbalanced weight rippling through his body, from the tension in his right hip on which he leans to his taut left arm.
Why the small penis? In classical art a large or even normal-sized packet was not deemed elegant, hence the daintier size.
And the big head and hands? *David* was designed to stand up high on a cathedral buttress in the apse, from where his head and hands would have appeared in perfect proportion.
Beauty treatments Body scrub with hydrochloric acid (1843); clay and cellulose pulp 'mud pack', bath in distilled water (2004).
Occupational hazards Over the centuries he's been struck by lightning, attacked by rioters and had his toes bashed with a hammer. The two pale white lines visible on his lower left arm is where his arm got broken during the 1527 revolt when the Medici were kicked out of Florence. Giorgio Vasari, then a child, picked up the pieces and 16 years later had them sent to Cosimo I who restored the statue, so the story goes.

Local Life

One-Stop Shop

Epicureans, follow Florence's foodie crowd to **Eataly** (055 015 36 01; www.eataly.net; Via de' Martelli 22r; 10am-10.30pm;), a one-stop culinary shop for everything Tuscan. Peruse beautifully arranged aisles laden with olive oils, conserved vegetables, pasta, rice, biscuits and so on. There are fresh bakery and deli counters, fridges laden with seemingly every cheese under the Italian sun and a coffee bar with outdoor seating. Many products are local and/or organic; most are by small producers. Upstairs is a wine cellar with 600 labels, a cooking school, summer terrace and the epicurean Osteria di Sopra serving lunch and dinner.

Midinette

FASHION & ACCESSORIES

25 Map p66, B4

From the shabby-chic floor – partly original tiles, partly bare paint – to the retro-inspired fashion, this French-stylist clothing and accessory boutique for women is impossibly romantic and creative. (www.midinette.firenze.it; Piazza della Stazione 51r; 10.30am-8pm Mon-Sat, 11am-8pm Sun)

Bartolini

HOMEWARES

26 Map p66, E4

Foodies with even the mildest interest in cooking will find Florence's most famous kitchen shop absolutely fascinating. Don't miss the collection of pasta-making tools. (055 29 14 97; www.dinobartolini.it; Via dei Servi 72r; 10am-7pm Mon-Sat)

Scarpelli Mosaici

ART

27 Map p66, D4

The entire Scarpelli family works hard to preserve the art of *pietre dure,* puzzle-like marble mosaics, at this lovely boutique and workshop tucked beneath a red-brick vaulted ceiling. If staff have time, they'll give you a quick introduction to this beautiful, yet incredibly painstaking, craft. (055 21 25 87; www.scarpellimosaici.it; Via Ricasoli 59r; 9.30am-6.30pm Mon-Fri, to 1pm Sat)

Understand

The Medici

Nowhere is a family name as linked with a city's identity as in Florence. Harking from the Mugello region north of Florence, the Medici were involved in the wool trade in the 13th and early 14th century. Though successful, they only came to prominence during the late 14th century, when Giovanni di Bicci de' Medici (1360–1429) established the Medici Bank. By the 15th century it was the largest in Europe. Giovanni's son Cosimo ('The Elder'; 1389–1464) used the vast family fortune to control local politics, becoming *gran maestro* (unofficial head of state) of the Florentine republic in 1434. A Humanist, he was an enlightened patron of Florentine culture and arts.

Cosimo's son Piero (1416–69) succeeded his father as *gran maestro* but didn't have his penchant for patronage or skill in politics. His son and heir Lorenzo ('The Magnificent'; 1449–92) fully embraced his grandfather's interest in politics and culture, but had no interest in the bank. After his death it became apparent that the bank was in financial trouble, a situation exacerbated by his incompetent son and heir Piero (1472–1503). Piero's short reign as *gran maestro* culminated in the dynasty's exile from Florence in 1494.

Lorenzo's reputation and wealth had ensured that his second son, Giovanni di Lorenzo de' Medici (1475–1521), attained a powerful position in the Church; he became pope in 1513 (as Leo X). His cousin Giulio de' Medici (1478–1535) followed in his footsteps, being elected pope in 1523 and taking the name Clement VII. Both continued the Medici tradition of arts patronage.The Medici returned to Florence in 1512, but few were as talented or successful as their forebears. The most impressive was Cosimo I (1519–74), an ambitious soldier who became Duke of Florence and then the first Grand Duke of Tuscany. He was also a great patron of the arts.

After the Medici's defeat by the House of Lorraine, Anna Maria Luisa de' Medici (1667–1743) willed the family's assets (including its magnificent art collection) to the Tuscan state, provided that nothing was ever removed from Florence.

Local Life
A Day in Fiesole

Getting There

🚌 **Bus** ATAF bus 7 (€1.20, 20 minutes, every 15 minutes) runs from Florence's Piazza San Marco up-hill to Fiesole's central square, Piazza Mino da Fiesole.

Set in cypress-studded hills 9km northeast of Florence, this bijou hilltop village has seduced visitors for centuries with its cool breezes, olive groves, Renaissance-styled villas and spectacular views. Before you arrive, download the map from the website of Fiesole's **tourist office** (📞055 596 13 11, 055 596 13 23; www.fiesoleforyou.it; Via Portigiani 3; ⏰10am-6.30pm summer, to 5.30pm winter). It shows three walking routes through the village, as well as tips for discovering the most breathtaking views of Florence.

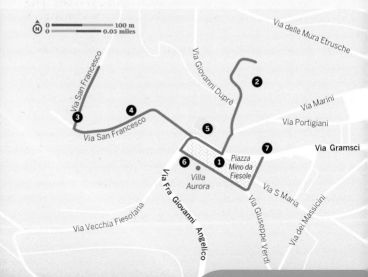

❶ Piazza People-Watching

Transport hub, *passeggiata* (evening stroll) hot spot and host to an antiques market on the first Sunday of each month, **Piazza Mino da Fiesole** is the village heart. Claim a stone bench or sit on a cafe terrace and watch the action unfold.

❷ Etruscan Ruins

Explore the **Area Archeologica** (www.museidifiesole.it; Via Portigiani 1; adult/reduced Fri-Sun €10/6; ⏰9am-7pm summer, shorter hours winter), a pretty site with ruins of an Etruscan temple (Fiesole was founded in the 7th century BC by the Etruscans), Roman baths, an archaeological museum with exhibits from the Bronze Age to the Roman period, and a 1st-century-BC Roman theatre where live music and theatre fill summer evenings during the **Estate Fiesolana** (June to August).

❸ Chiesa e Convento di San Francesco

Hike up steep, walled, pedestrian **Via San Francesco** and be blown away by the staggeringly beautiful panorama of Florence that unfolds from the terrace adjoining this 15th-century **church** (Via San Francesco; ⏰9am-noon & 3-6pm) and former convent at the top.

❹ Lunch with View

Feast on hypnotic views and delicious Tuscan cuisine on the panoramic terrace of **La Reggia degli Etruschi** (📞055 5 93 85; www.lareggiadeglietruschi.com; Via San Francesco; meals €30; ⏰7-9.30pm Mon-Wed, 12.30-1.30pm & 7-9.30pm Thu-Sun), halfway down the hill and abuzz with weekending Florentines.

❺ Cattedrale di San Romolo

Continue down the hill and seek some cool air in Fiesole's **cathedral** (Piazza Mino da Fiesole; admission free; ⏰7.30am-noon & 3-5pm), begun in the 11th century. A glazed terracotta statue of San Romolo by Giovanni della Robbia guards the entrance inside.

❻ An Afternoon Drink

Enjoy an *aperitivo* at **JJ Hill** (📞055 5 93 24; Piazza Mino da Fiesole 40; ⏰6pm-midnight Mon-Wed, 5pm-1am Thu-Sat, 5-11pm Sun), an Irish pub with a tip-top beer list. Or lounge on the more refined, pagoda-covered terrace of **Villa Aurora** (📞055 5 93 63; www.villaaurorafiesole.com; Piazza Mino da Fiesole 39; meals €30; ⏰noon-2.30pm & 7-10.30pm), a favourite for its romantic Florence view since 1860.

❼ A Sunset Bike Ride

Fire up the romantic in you with a 2½-hour, 21km guided bike ride (€50 including bike hire) by sunset back to Florence with **FiesoleBike** (📞345 3350926; www.fiesolebike.it), a creative bike rental/guiding outfit run with passion by local Fiesole lad Giovanni Crescioli (a qualified biking and hiking guide to boot). His 'sunset' tour departs daily from Piazza Mino da Fiesole at 5pm in season; book in advance online.

Explore

Santa Croce

Despite being only a hop, skip and jump from the city's major museums, this ancient part of Florence is far removed from the tourist maelstrom. The streets behind the basilica are home to plenty of locals, all of whom seem to be taking their neighbourhood's reinvention as hipster central – epicentre of the city's bar and club scene – with remarkable aplomb.

The Sights in a Day

Begin with breakfast and glorious coffee at third-wave coffee shop **Ditta Artigianale** (p96), then head to the **Museo del Bargello** (p86) to admire Renaissance Tuscan sculptures. Visit on a sunny day when the natural sun rays flood the vintage, dimly lit exhibition rooms and their incredible bounty of sculptures in an intoxicating light; true Michelangelo aficionados must continue to **Museo Casa Buonarroti** (p91).

Meander east to bijou, village-like Piazza Sant' Ambrogio with its neighbouring open-air food market, **Mercato di Sant'Ambrogio** (p92), and cluster of famous Florentine eating addresses. Grab a sandwich at **Semel** (p92) or lunch with locals at busy no-frills **Il Giova** (p94). Devote the afternoon to the neighbourhood's star turn, **Basilica di Santa Croce** (p84).

Begin the evening with a customary *aperitivo* (pre-dinner drink with nibbles) over Tuscan salami at **All'Antico Vinaio** (p91). Indulge in gastronomic brilliance at **Enoteca Pinchiorri** (p93), fish at fashionable **Vivo** (p92) or thin-crust Neapolitan pizza at trendy **Santarpia** (p92).

For a local's night out in Santa Croce, see p88.

Top Sights

Basilica di Santa Croce (p84)

Museo del Bargello (p86)

Local Life

A Night Out in Santa Croce (p88)

Best of Florence

Eating

Trattoria Cibrèo (p92)

Vivoli (p94)

Trippaio Sergio Pollini (p93)

La Toraia (p95)

Drinking

Ditta Artigianale (p96)

Le Murate Caffè Letterario (p94)

Nightlife

Il Teatro del Sale (p89)

Bamboo (p89)

Full Up (p95)

Getting There

Walk From Piazza della Stazione walk southeast via Via de' Panzani, Via de' Cerretani and Via del Proconsolo to Museo del Bargello. Take Via Ghibellina and turn right at Via Giuseppe Verdi to Piazza di Santa Croce.

Top Sights
Basilica di Santa Croce

The austere interior of this massive Franciscan basilica is a surprise when compared with its magnificent neo-Gothic facade, which is enlivened by varying shades of coloured marble. Though most visitors come to see the tombs of Michelangelo, Dante, Galileo and Machiavelli in the nave, it's the Giotto frescoes and the utterly exquisite Cappella de' Pazzi that are the real highlights.

Map p90, C3

055 246 61 05

www.santacroceopera.it

Piazza di Santa Croce

adult/reduced €8/4

9.30am-5.30pm Mon-Sat, 2-5.30pm Sun

Frescoed Chapels

Giotto's murals feature John the Baptist in the **Cappella Peruzzi** (1310–20), while the **Cappella Bardi** (1320-28) features scenes from the life of St Francis. Giotto's assistant and loyal pupil, Taddeo Gaddi, frescoed **Cappella Majeure** (currently being restored) and **Cappella Baroncelli** (1328–38).

Sagrestia

From the transept chapels, a doorway designed by Michelozzo leads into a corridor, off which is the enchanting 14th-century Sacristy with Taddeo Gaddi's fresco of the Crucifixion. The large painted wooden cross (c 1288) by Cimabue was one of many artworks to be damaged in the 1966 floods which inundated Santa Croce in more than 4m of water.

Cappella de' Pazzi

Backtrack to the church and follow the 'Uscita' (exit) sign, opposite the main entrance, to access the basilica's two serene cloisters designed by Brunelleschi. His unfinished Cappella de' Pazzi is notable for its harmonious lines and restrained terracotta medallions of the Apostles by Luca della Robbia, and is a masterpiece of Renaissance architecture.

Cenacolo

Continue to the second cloister. Inside the cavernous Refectory, Taddeo Gaddi's dazzling *The Last Supper* (1334–56) fills the entire far wall, but it's Georgio Vasari's *The Last Supper* (1546) that steals the show. Submerged in floodwater for at least 12 hours, the severely damaged oil painting was returned to Santa Croce following 50 years of restoration in 2016.

☑ **Top Tips**

▶ Walk through the church bookshop to access the **Scuola del Cuoio**, a traditional leather school where you can see bags being fashioned and buy the finished products.

▶ In 1817 the French writer Stendhal experienced a racing heartbeat, nausea and dizziness when exiting the basilica. His reaction to its cultural richness (and that of Florence as a whole) has been shared by many other visitors, hence the description 'Stendhal Syndrome'. Consider yourself warned.

✕ **Take a Break**

Join locals for a quick tasty trattoria lunch at Il Giova (p94).

For an *aperitivo* (predinner drink), head to one of the many bars on Via de' Benci.

Top Sights
Museo del Bargello

It was from fortress-like Palazzo del Bargello – built in the mid-13th century and Florence's oldest still-standing public building – that the podestà meted out justice until 1502. Today, the building safeguards Italy's most comprehensive collection of Tuscan Renaissance sculpture, including Michelangelo's best early works. While crowds clamour to see his *David*, few rush here – rendering the Bargello a highly rewarding experience.

👁 Map p90, A2

www.bargellomusei.
beniculturali.it

Via del Proconsolo 4

adult/reduced €8/4

⏱ 8.15am-1.50pm, closed 2nd & 4th Sun, 1st, 3rd & 5th Mon of month

Courtyard and Salone di Donatello

Michelangelo

Michelangelo was just 21 when he created the drunken, grape-adorned Bacchus (1496–97) displayed in the ground-floor **Sala di Michelangelo e della Scultura del Cinque Cento** (first door on the right after entering the interior courtyard from the ticket office). Other Michelangelo works include the marble bust of *Brutus* (c 1539–40), the *David/Apollo* (1530–32) and the large, uncompleted roundel of the *Madonna and Child with the Infant St John* (1503–05; aka the *Tondo Pitti*).

Salone di Donatello

The majestic salon where the city's general council met now showcases works by Donatello and other 15th-century sculptors. Don't miss his *St George* (1416–17), originally on the facade of Chiesa di Orsanmichele and now within a tabernacle at the hall's far end, which brought a new sense of perspective and movement to Italian sculpture.

Yet it is Donatello's two versions of *David,* a favourite subject for sculptors, that really fascinate: Donatello fashioned his slender, youthful dressed image in marble in 1408 and his fabled bronze between 1439 and 1443. The latter is extraordinary – the more so when you consider it was the first free-standing naked statue to be sculpted since classical times.

The Della Robbias

The 2nd floor moves into the 16th century with a superb collection of terracotta pieces by the prolific della Robbia family, including Andrea's *Ritratto idealizia di fanciullo* (*Bust of a Boy*; c 1475) and Giovanni's *Pietà* (1514). Instantly recognisable, Giovanni's works are more flamboyant than those of his father Luca or cousin Andrea, using a larger palette of colours.

☑ **Top Tips**

▶ Don't try to visit the Bargello and Uffizi together – their collections are too large and important to cram into a single day.

▶ Michelangelo devotees can follow a chronological trail of his sculptural works in Florence by visiting *David* at the Galleria dell'Accademia, stopping at the Museo delle Cappelle Medicee to view the sculptures in the Sagrestia Nuova and then heading to the Bargello to admire his second *David* (aka Apollo) and the *Tondo Pitti*. End with family home, Casa Buonarroti.

✕ **Take a Break**

Continue the arty theme with a coffee break, light lunch or afternoon tea at hipster cafe-bookshop Brac (p93).

Grab a quick *panino* or linger over a traditional Tuscan meal at Antico Noè (p94).

Local Life
A Night Out in Santa Croce

In this heavily touristed city, it can be hard to find authentic pockets of local life. Fortunately, the fact that the basilica is the only top-drawer sight in Santa Croce means the neighbourhood is blessedly bereft of sightseers – locals flock here to shop, eat, drink and party with their fellow Florentines as a result.

1 Riverside Lounging

Begin the night out the Florentine way – soaking up the light, view and mood from a bridge across the Arno. Lounge with locals on **Ponte alle Grazie** as the sun softens and turns the river's romantic cascade of bridges a hazy mellow pink.

2 Shopping at Dusk

Nose-dive into trendy Via de' Benci with its bevy of bars and boutiques.

Pop into **Boutique Nadine** (📞055 247 82 74; www.boutiquenadine.com; Via de' Benci 32r; ⏱2.30-7.30pm Mon, 10.30am-7.30pm Tue-Sat, 2-7.30pm Sun) to browse its vintage clothing, jewellery, homewares and pretty little trinkets displayed in antique cabinets. Continue to the chic fashion boutiques of **Via del Proconsolo**.

❸ Fishing Lab

End your shopping spree with an *aperitivo* (pre-dinner drink) in the company of fried anchovies, tuna buns and other delightfully fishy nibbles at **Fishing Lab** (📞055 24 06 18; www. fishinglab.it; Via del Proconsolo 16r; meals €40; ⏱11am-midnight). Peek upstairs at the fragments of 14th- and 15th-century frescoes decorating the enchanting, vaulted dining room.

❹ Don Your Dancing Shoes

Dance with beautiful Florentine hipsters at **Bamboo** (📞339 4298764; www. bambooloungeclub.com; Via Giuseppe Verdi 59r; ⏱7pm-4am Fri, Sat & Mon, to 3am Thu), a lounge and dance club with chintzy red seating and a mix of hip-hop and R&B on the turntable. Dress up and look good to get in. (The dress code, if it helps, is 'smart, casual, sexy, chic.')

❺ Post-Midnight Party

Check out the post-midnight party at **Caffè Sant'Ambrogio** (📞055 247 72 77; Piazza Sant'Ambrogio 7r; ⏱10am-3am; 📶), one of Santa Croce's original, iconic hang-outs. Trendy 30-something Florentines flock here for after-work cocktails, late-night drinks and parties 'til dawn.

❻ Il Teatro del Sale

No Florentine chef is more charismatic than Fabio Picchi, whose eccentric **Il Teatro del Sale** (📞055 200 14 92; www. teatrodelsale.com; Via dei Macci 111r; lunch/ dinner/weekend brunch €15/35/20; ⏱11am-3pm & 7.30-11pm Tue-Sat, 11am-3pm Sun, closed Aug) guarantees an unforgettable experience. Dinner is a hectic, mesmerising symphony of outstanding Tuscan dishes, culminating at 9.30pm in a live performance of drama, music or comedy arranged by Picchi's wife, comic actress Maria Cassi.

❼ Monkey Bar

By midnight there's a nip in the air. Duck into **Monkey Bar** (📞055 24 28 62; www.facebook.com/MonkeyBarFirenze; Via della Mattonaia 20r; ⏱6pm-2am), a noisy pub packed with Florentine and foreign students downing shots, Spritz and well-made Bloody Marys.

❽ Late-Night Drinks

Show over, plunge into the star-lit night and follow the hip crowd to **Largo Pietro Annigoni**. This large, car-free plaza opposite the Sant'Ambrogio market buzzes with life on summer nights when its bounty of alfresco terraces, including **Drogheria** (📞055 247 88 69; www.drogheriafirenze. it; Largo Pietro Annigoni 22; ⏱10am-3am), overflow with late-night drinkers.

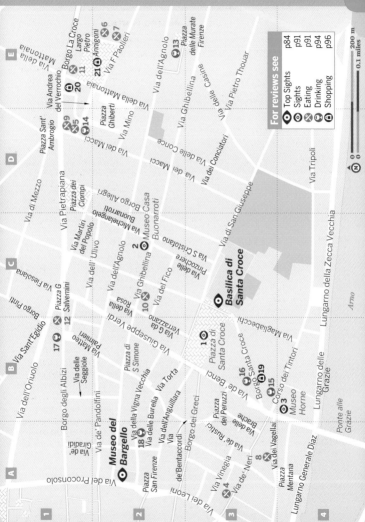

200 m
0.1 miles

Via della Mattonaia

Borgo La Croce

Largo Pietro Annigoni 6
Via F Paolieri 7

21 11
20

Piazza dell'Agnolo 13
Piazza delle Murate Firenze

Via dell'Agnolo

Via della Mattonaia

Piazza Sant' Ambrogio

9 5
14

Piazza Ghiberti

Via Mino

Via dei Macci

Via delle Casine

Via Ghibellina

Via Pietro Thouar

Via di Mezzo

Via Pietrapiana

Piazza dei Ciompi

Via Martiri del Popolo

Via dell'Ulivo

Via dell'Agnolo

Borgo Allegri

Via Michelangelo Buonarroti

2 Museo Casa Buonarroti

Via S Cristofano

Via dei Macci

Via delle Conce

Via dei Conciatori

Via di San Giuseppe

Via Tripoli

Via Fiesolana

Borgo Pinti

Piazza G Salvemini

Via dell'Oriuolo

Via Sant'Egidio

17

12

Via Matteo Palmieri

Via delle Seggiole

Piazza di S Simone

Via della Rosa

Via del Fico

Via della Pinzochere

Via Ghibellina

10

Via G da Verrazzano

Basilica di Santa Croce

◆ Basilica di Santa Croce

Lungarno della Zecca Vecchia

Arno

Via de' Pandolfini

Borgo degli Albizi

Via de' Giraldi

Via de' Pandolfini

18

Via della Vigna Vecchia

Via delle Burella

Via dell'Anguillara

Via Torta

Via de' Bentaccordi

Borgo dei Greci

Via Giuseppe Verdi

Piazza di Santa Croce

1

16
19
15

Borgo Santa Croce

Corso dei Tintori

Via Magliabechi

Lungarno delle Grazie

◆ Museo del Bargello

Via del Proconsolo

Piazza San Firenze

Via dei Leoni

Piazza dei Peruzzi

Via de' Rustici

Via delle Brache

Via de' Benci

3 Museo Horne

Piazza Mentana

Via Vinegia

Via de' Neri

Via dei Vagellai

8

4

Lungarno Generale Diaz

Ponte alle Grazie

Sights

Piazza di Santa Croce
PIAZZA

1 ◉ Map p90, B3

This square was cleared in the Middle Ages to allow the faithful to gather when the church itself was full. In Savonarola's day, heretics were executed here. Such an open space inevitably found other uses, and from the 14th century it was often the colourful scene of jousts, festivals and *calcio storico* (www.calciostorico.it) matches. The city's 2nd-century amphitheatre took up the area facing the square's western end: Piazza dei Peruzzi, Via de' Bentaccordi and Via Torta mark the oval outline of its course.

Museo Casa Buonarroti
MUSEUM

2 ◉ Map p90, C2

Though Michelangelo never lived in Casa Buonarroti, his heirs devoted some of the artist's hard-earned wealth to the construction of this 17th-century *palazzo* (mansion) to honour his memory. The little museum contains frescoes of the artist's life and two of his most important early works – the serene, bas-relief *Madonna of the Stairs* and the unfinished *Battle of the Centaurs*. (☏055 24 17 52; www.casabuonarroti.it; Via Ghibellina 70; adult/reduced €6.40/4.50; ⊙10am-5pm Wed-Mon, to 4pm Nov-Feb)

Museo Horne
MUSEUM

3 ◉ Map p90, B4

One of the many eccentric Brits who made Florence home in the early 20th century, Herbert Percy Horne bought and renovated this Renaissance *palazzo*, then installed his eclectic collection of 14th- and 15th-century Italian art, ceramics, furniture and other oddments. There are a few works by masters such as Giotto and Filippo Lippi. More interesting is the furniture, some of which is exquisite. (☏055 24 46 61; www.museohorne.it; Via de' Benci 6; adult/reduced €7/5; ⊙9am-1pm Mon-Sat)

Eating

All'Antico Vinaio
OSTERIA €

4 ✕ Map p90, A3

The crowd spills out the door of this noisy Florentine thoroughbred. Push your way to the tables at the back to taste cheese and salami in situ (reservations recommended). Or join the queue at the deli counter for a well-stuffed focaccia wrapped in waxed paper to take away – the quality is outstanding. Pour yourself a glass of wine while you wait. (☏055 238 27 23; www.allanticovinaio.com; Via de' Neri 65r; tasting platters €10-30; ⊙10am-4pm & 6-11pm Tue-Sat, noon-3.30pm Sun)

◯ Local Life
Lunch at the Market

Florentines swear by **Semel** (Piazza Ghiberti 44r; panini €3.50-5; ⊙11.30am-3pm Mon-Sat), a pocket-sized sandwich bar with no fixed menu, rather an impossible-to-decide choice of six gourmet combos, crafted with love by passionate owner and *panini* king Marco Paparozzi. Wash it down with a glass of water or wine, and pride yourself on snagging one of the tastiest lunches in town.

For *dolci* (dessert), nip across the street to buy some local, seasonal fruit at the **Mercato di Sant'Ambrogio** (Map p90, D2; Piazza Ghiberti; ⊙7am-2pm Mon-Sat), the neighbourhood's bustling outdoor food market with an intimate, local flavour. The best day is Saturday when farmers from the region travel here to sell their produce straight from the field.

Trattoria Cibrèo   TUSCAN €€

 Map p90, D1

Dine at chez Fabio Picchi and you'll instantly understand why a queue gathers outside before it opens. Once inside, revel in top-notch Tuscan cuisine: perhaps *pappa al pomodoro* (a thick soupy mash of tomato, bread and basil) followed by *polpettine di pollo e ricotta* (chicken and ricotta meatballs). No reservations, no credit cards, no pasta and arrive early to snag a table. (www.cibreo.com; Via dei

Macci 122r; meals €40; ⊙12.50-2.30pm & 6.50-11pm Tue-Sat, closed Aug)

Santarpia   PIZZA €

 Map p90, E2

Florentines can't get enough of the thin-crust Neapolitan pizzas oven-fired by master *pizzaiolo* (pizza chef) Giovanni Santarpia at his thoroughly contemporary pizzeria across the road from Mercato di Sant'Ambrogio. Grab a table between brightly spangled walls and open the feast with deep-fried *baccalà* (salted cod), porcini mushrooms or other *fritto* – there is even *pizza fritta con lampredotto* (deep-fried pizza with tripe). (☎055 24 58 29; www.santarpia.biz; Largo Pietro Annigoni 9; pizza €8.50-11; ⊙7.30pm-midnight Wed-Mon; 🛜)

Vivo   FISH €€

 Map p90, E2

Raw fish, shellfish, oysters and other fishy dishes – all caught in waters around Italy by the Manno family's 30-strong fleet of fishing boats – are cooked up by female chef Anna Maria at this fish restaurant, inside a hangar-styled contemporary space with a fishing-boat-shaped bar. Everything is ultra fresh and the daily changing menu includes many a rare or forgotten fish. (☎333 1824183; www.ristorante vivo.it; Largo Pietro Annigoni 9a/b; seafood platters €15-50, meals €45; ⊙12.30-2.30pm & 7.30-11pm Tue-Sun; 🛜)

Understand

Understand
Calcio Storico

It might well have been conceived to accommodate congregation overspill from the basilica, but it was inevitable that a space as vast and open as Piazza di Santa Croce would find other uses, too. Jousts and festivals have been staged here since the 14th century, as have matches of *calcio storico* (www.calciostoricofiorentino.it), a traditional sport that is a cross between football and rugby. This Florentine favourite pits 27 very burly men in brightly coloured costumes who beat each other bloody (literally) as they try to move the ball up and down the pitch. Sucker-punching and kicks to the head are forbidden, but few other rules apply – headbutting, punching, elbowing and choking are allowed. Games are played on the square each year during Florence's Festa di San Giovanni (24 June).

Look for the marble stone embedded in the wall below the gaily frescoed facade of Palazzo dell'Antella, on the south side of Piazza di Santa Croce; it marks the halfway line on what is essentially one of the oldest football pitches in the world.

Brac   VEGETARIAN €

8 Map p90, A3

This hipster cafe-bookshop – a hybrid dining-*aperitivi* address – cooks up inventive, home-style and strictly vegetarian and/or vegan cuisine. Its decor is recycled vintage with the occasional kid's drawing thrown in for that intimate homey touch; and the vibe is artsy. (📞055 094 48 77; www.libreriabrac.net; Via dei Vagellai 18r; meals €20; ⏱noon-midnight, closed 2 weeks mid-Aug; 🛜🖍)

Trippaio Sergio Pollini   FAST FOOD €

9 Map p90, D1

For a fast munch-on-the-move follow Florentines to this *trippaio* (mobile tripe stand) for a tripe *panino* (sandwich). Think cow's stomach chopped up, boiled, sliced, bunged between bread and doused in *salsa verde* (pea-green sauce of smashed parsley, garlic, capers and anchovies). A bastion of good old-fashioned Florentine tradition, this *trippaio* is one of the city's busiest. (Piazza Sant' Ambrogio; tripe €3.50; ⏱9.30am-3pm Mon, to 8pm Tue-Sat)

Enoteca Pinchiorri   TUSCAN €€€

10 Map p90, C2

Niçois chef Annie Féolde applies French techniques to her versions of refined Tuscan cuisine and does it so well that this is the only restaurant in Tuscany to brandish three shiny Michelin stars. The setting is a 16th-century palace hotel and the wine list is mind-boggling in its extent

Local Life
An Afternoon Gelato

Florentines take their gelato seriously and there's healthy rivalry among the operators of local *gelaterie artigianale* (shops selling handmade gelato), who strive to create the city's creamiest, most flavourful and freshest ice cream using seasonal flavours. In Santa Croce, **Vivoli** (☎055 29 23 34; www.vivoli.it; Via dell'Isola delle Stinche 7; tubs €2-10; ⏰7.30am-midnight Tue-Sat, 9am-midnight Sun, to 9pm winter) is the gelateria with the greatest number of devotees. Pay at the cash desk then trade your receipt for the good stuff. No cones, only tubs, plus – unusually for a gelateria – coffee, cakes and comfy inside seating too.

and excellence. A once-in-a-lifetime experience. Reserve in advance. (☎055 24 27 77; www.enotecapinchiorri.com; Via Ghibellina 87r; 4-/7-/8-course tasting menu €150/225/275; ⏰lunch & dinner Tue-Sat, closed Aug)

Il Giova
TRATTORIA €

 11 ✖ Map p90, E1

Pocket-sized and packed, this cheery trattoria with marigold walls and colourful ceramic-tiled tables is everything a traditional Florentine eating place should be. Dig into century-old dishes like *zuppa della nonna* (grandma's soup), *risotto del giorno* (risotto of the day) or *mafalde al ragù* (long-ribboned pasta with meat sauce)

and pride yourself on having found the locals' lunchtime canteen. (☎055 248 06 39; www.ilgiova.com; Borgo La Croce 73r; meals €15; ⏰noon-3pm & 7-11pm Mon-Sat)

Antico Noè
OSTERIA €€

12 ✖ Map p90, B1

Don't be put off by the dank alley in which you'll find this old butcher's shop with marble-clad walls, wrought-iron meat hooks and a name inspired by an old Italian vermouth. The drunks loitering outside are generally harmless and the down-to-earth Tuscan fodder served is a real joy. For a quick bite, grab a *panino* (€4.50 to €5) at its *fiaschetteria* (small tavern). (http://anticonoe.com/; Volta di San Piero 6r; meals €40; ⏰noon-2am Mon & Wed-Sat)

Drinking

Le Murate Caffè Letterario
BAR, CAFE

13 🍷 Map p90, E2

This artsy cafe-bar in Florence's former jail is where literati meet to talk, create and perform over coffee, drinks and light meals. The literary cafe hosts everything from readings and interviews with authors – Florentine, Italian and international – to film screenings, debates, live music and art exhibitions. Tables are built from recycled window frames and in summer everything spills outside into the brick courtyard. (☎055 234 68 72; www.lemurate.it; Piazza delle Murate Firenze; ⏰9am-1am; 🛜)

Caffè Cibrèo

CAFE

14 Map p90, D1

The cafe arm of Florentine super-star chef Fabio Picci, this charming old-world cafe behind Mercato di Sant'Ambrogio is an idyllic spot for a mid-morning coffee and sugar-dusted *ciambella* (doughnut ring). (055 234 58 53; Via Andrea del Verrocchio 5; ⏱8am-1am Tue-Sat, closed Aug)

Beer House Club

CRAFT BEER

15 Map p90, B3

Sample the best of Italian craft beer at this young, fun beer bar in Santa Croce. Pick from 10 craft beers on tap and another 100 bottled beers, local, Italian and international. Big sports matches are screened here, the bar has a party-packed social agenda – check

Local Life
Riverside Street Food

'Bringing the countryside to the city' is the driver behind **La Toraia** (338 5367198; www.latoraia.com; Lungarno del Tempio; burger €6, with cheese €7; ⏱noon-midnight 15 Apr–15 Oct), a cherry-red artisan food truck whose name translates as 'breeding shed'. Parked riverside, a 15-minute stroll east of Piazza di Santa Croce, the truck cooks up sweet 140g burgers, crafted from tender Chianina meat sourced at the family farm in Val di Chiana and topped with melted *pecorino* (sheep's milk cheese).

its Facebook page for events – and it serves food. (055 247 67 63; www.beerhouseclub.eu; Corso dei Tintori 34r; ⏱noon-3am)

Quelo

BAR

16 Map p90, B3

Hidden down a rather dark and dank street near Basilica di Santa Croce, this tiny bar is a sweet spot for a quick drink between sights or a dusk-time *aperitivo* with generous buffet spread. Check its Facebook page for upcoming DJ sets, live music and other cultural happenings. Interior design is 1950s vintage. (055 1999 1474; Borgo Santa Croce 15r; ⏱8.30am-2am; 📶)

Lion's Fountain

IRISH PUB

17 Map p90, B1

If you have the urge to hear more English than Italian – or to hear local bands play for that matter – this is the place. On a pretty pedestrian square, Florence's busiest Irish pub buzzes in summer when the beer-loving crowd spills across most of the square. Live music and a canary-yellow food 'truck' serving burgers, nachos, clubs, wings and brunch (€5 to €10). (055 234 44 12; www.thelionsfountain.com; Borgo degli Albizi 34r; ⏱10am-3am)

Full Up

CLUB

18 Map p90, A2

A variety of sounds energises the crowd at this popular Florentine nightclub, in the biz since 1958, where

Q Local Life

Third-Wave Coffee & Gin

With industrial decor and a welcoming, laid-back vibe, **Ditta Artigianale** (Map p90, A3; ✆055 274 15 41; www.dittaartigianale.it; Via de' Neri 32r; ⏰8am-10pm Sun-Thu, 8am-midnight Fri, 9.30am-midnight Sat; 🛜) – an ingenious coffee roastery and gin bar – is a perfect place to hang any time of day. The creation of three-times Italian barista champion Francesco Sanapo, it's famed for its first-class coffee and outstanding gin cocktails. If you're yearning for a flat white, cold brew tonic or cappuccino made with almond, soy or coconut milk, come here.

Fantastic food is served all day, kicking off with Greek yoghurt and muesli, French toast and pancake breakfasts from 9am and culminating with tasty tapas from 7pm when a gourmet *aperitivo* kicks in.

20-somethings dance until dawn. (✆055 29 30 06; www.fullupclub.com; Via della Vigna Vecchia 21r; ⏰11pm-4am Thu-Sat, closed Aug)

Shopping

Aquaflor   COSMETICS

19 🔒 Map p90, B3

This elegant Santa Croce perfumery in a vaulted 15th-century *palazzo* exudes romance and exoticism. Artisan scents are crafted here with tremendous care and precision by master perfumer Sileno Cheloni, who works with precious essences from all over the world, including Florentine iris. Organic soaps, cosmetics and body-care products make equally lovely gifts to take back home. (✆055 234 34 71; www.florenceparfum.com; Borgo Santa Croce 6; ⏰10am-7pm)

Alla Sosta dei Papi   FOOD & DRINKS

20 🔒 Map p90, E1

This tiny *enoteca* (wine bar) is a wine-buff one-stop shop. Tuscan wines range from as cheap as chips (bring your own bottle and fill it up for €2.40 per litre) to the very best. Even better, taste before you buy over a glass in the company of cheese and salami platters, crostini and other mouthwatering wine-bar-style nibbles. (✆055 234 11 74; www.sostadeipapi.it; Borgo La Croce 81r; ⏰4-10pm Mon, 9am-1.30pm & 4-10pm Tue-Sat)

Mercato delle Pulci   ANTIQUES

21 🔒 Map p90, E2

Historically at home (alongside the city's fish market) on Piazza dei Ciompi since 1900, Florence's antiques and flea market can be found for the moment opposite Santa Croce's Mercato di Sant'Ambrogio. Peruse its racing-green stalls for a piece of Old Tuscany to take home. (Flea Market; Largo Pietro Annigoni; ⏰9am-7.30pm)

Understand

Florentine Cuisine

Be it by sinking your teeth into a flavoursome *bistecca alla fiorentina* (T-bone steak), savouring the taste and aroma of freshly shaved white truffles or sampling rustic specialities such as *trippa alla fiorentina* (tripe slow-cooked with onion, carrot, celery and tomatoes), you're sure to discover plenty of taste sensations when eating in Florence.

Florentine cuisine has stayed faithful to its humble regional roots, relying on fresh local produce and eschewing fussy execution. That's not to say that it lacks refinement – Florence is home to many highly skilled and internationally lauded chefs – but it's true to say that the hallmark of the local cuisine is its simplicity.

When here, be sure to try a *bistecca alla fiorentina,* but be prepared for it to come to the table *al sangue* (bloody). Accompanied by slow-cooked white beans, or sometimes roast potatoes, this signature dish relies on the quality of its Chianina beef (from the Val di Chiana south of Florence) and the skill with which it has been butchered and grilled. Wash it down with a Tuscan red wine – a Chianti Classico, Brunello di Montepulciano or perhaps even a Vino Nobile di Montepulciano.

Other local specialities include *cinghiale* (wild boar), best savoured in autumnal stews; antipasti plates featuring fresh *pecorino* cheese made from sheep's milk, locally cured meats and crostini (lightly toasted pieces of bread topped with liver pâté); and *minestre* (soups) including *zuppa di fagioli* (bean soup), *ribollita* (a 'reboiled' bean, vegetable and bread soup with black cabbage) and *pappa al pomodoro* (a thick bread and tomato soup).

Adventurous eaters need go no further than the city's *trippai* (tripe carts), where tripe *panini* (sandwiches) are doused in *salsa verde* (a tasty pea-green sauce of smashed parsley, garlic, capers and anchovies). Such rustic, powerfully flavoured treats stand in stark contrast to the refined joy of white truffles from San Miniato near Pisa – best shaved over a bowl of pasta or risotto – and porcini mushrooms gathered in local forests and tossed through *taglierini* (thin ribbon pasta). Both of these indulgences are surprisingly affordable and utterly delectable.

Explore

Boboli & San Miniato al Monte

If you start to suffer museum overload (a common occurrence in this culturally resplendent city), you may decide that it's important to stretch your legs and see some sky. If so, the tier of palaces, villas and gardens ascending to the Basilica di San Miniato al Monte, one of the city's oldest and most beautiful churches, will fit the bill perfectly.

The Sights in a Day

☼ Devote the morning to the galleries and garden of the monumental **Palazzo Pitti** (p100), home at various times to members of the powerful Medici, Lorraine and Savoy families. End in the magnificent **Giardino di Boboli** (p103), not missing the romantic view of quintessential Tuscany that pops into view from the terrace by the **Museo delle Porcellane** (p103).

☼ Enjoy the green stroll to **Giardino Bardini** (pictured left; p106). Visit its garden and enjoy lunch with a view at **La Leggenda dei Frati** (p107), reserve a table in advance. Afterwards, walk through village-like **San Niccolò**: shop for bespoke perfume at **Lorenzo Villoresi** (p110); get acquainted with street artist **Clet** (p110); scale **Torre San Niccolò** (p106) for beautiful city views. Then hike uphill to Romanesque gem, **Basilica di San Miniato al Monte** (p106).

☾ Watch the sun set over Florence from **Piazzale Michelangelo** (p106), then meander downhill for an *aperitivo* (pre-dinner drink) at **ZEB** (p108) or **Le Volpi e l'Uva** (p109). From here, the perennially popular restaurants, lounge bars and fashionable cocktail bars of the **Oltrarno** (p122) are a short walk away.

◉ Top Sight
Palazzo Pitti (p100)

♥ Best of Florence

Views

Piazzale Michelangelo (p106)

Basilica di San Miniato al Monte (p106)

La Leggenda dei Frati (p107)

La Loggia (p109)

Torre San Niccolò (p106)

San Niccolò 39 (p108)

Eating

La Leggenda dei Frati (p107)

Drinking

Le Volpi e l'Uva (p109)

Flò (p109)

Getting There

🚶 **Walk** From Piazza della Stazione walk southeast along Via de' Panzani and Via de' Cerretani to theDuomo. Head down Via Roma, cross Ponte Vecchio and continue south along Via Guicciardini to Palazzo Pitti.

🚌 **Bus** Bus 13 runs to Piazzale Michelangelo.

Top Sights
Palazzo Pitti

Wealthy banker Luca Pitti commissioned Brunelleschi to design this palace in 1457, but once completed, waning family fortunes forced it to be sold to arch-rivals, the Medici. It subsequently became home to the dukes of Lorraine and, when Florence was made capital of the nascent Kingdom of Italy in 1865, the Savoy (who gave it to the state in 1919).

Map p104, C2

www.polomuseale.firenze.it

Piazza dei Pitti

8.15am-6.50pm Tue-Sun

Tesoro dei Granduchi

Exquisite amber carvings, ivory miniatures, glittering tiaras and headpieces, silver pillboxes and various other gems and jewels are displayed in the elaborately frescoed Grand Dukes' Treasury, on the ground floor of Palazzo Pitti. Notable (but not always open) is the **Sala di Giovanni da San Giovanni**, which sports lavish head-to-toe frescoes (1635–42) celebrating the life of Lorenzo Il Magnifico – spot Michelangelo giving Lorenzo a statue. 'Talk little, be brief and witty' is the curt motto above the painted staircase in the next room, the public audience chamber, where the grand duke received visitors in the presence of his court.

Galleria d'Arte Moderna

By 'modern', the Pitti's powers-that-be mean 18th and 19th century. So forget about Marini, Mertz or Clemente – the collection of this 2nd-floor gallery is dominated by late-19th-century works by artists of the Florentine Macchiaioli school (the local equivalent of impressionism), including Telemaco Signorini (1835–1901) and Giovanni Fattori (1825–1908).

Museo della Moda e del Costume

Pitti's Fashion and Costume Museum features an absolutely fascinating, if somewhat macabre, display of the semidecomposed burial clothes of Cosimo I, his wife Eleonora di Toledo and their son Don Garzia. Considering the fact that they were buried for centuries, Eleonora's gown and silk stockings are remarkably preserved, as are Cosimo's satin doublet and wool breeches and Garzia's doublet, beret and short cape.

Appartamenti Reali

Accessed through the **Galleria Palatina**, these Royal Apartments are presented as they were c 1880–91 when the palace was occupied by members of the House of Savoy. The style and division

---

☑ Top Tips

▶ Ticketing for the palace complex and surrounding gardens is complicated: choose from Ticket 1 (Galleria Palatina, Appartamenti Reali and Galleria d'Arte Moderna); Ticket 2 (Museo della Moda e del Costume, Museo degli Argenti, Giardino di Boboli, Giardino Bardini and Museo delle Porcellane); and Ticket 3 (all sights; valid for three days). Buy these from the ticket office to the right of the palace entrance.

✗ Take a Break

In summer, indulge in a lunch of a lifetime at Michelin-starred La Leggenda dei Frati (p107) in the gardens of Villa Bardini – views from the stone loggia overlooking the Florentine skyline are impossibly romantic.

In winter, enjoy a classic Tuscan meal at family-run Da Ruggero (p108).

of tasks assigned to each space is reminiscent of Spanish royal palaces, and all are heavily bedecked with drapes, silk and chandeliers.

Galleria Palatina

Raphaels and Rubens vie for centre stage in the enviable collection of 16th- to 18th-century art amassed by the Medici and Lorraine dukes in this art gallery, reached by several flights of stairs from the palace's central courtyard. This gallery has retained the original display arrangement of paintings (squeezed in, often on top of each other), so can be visually overwhelming – go slow and focus on the works one by one.

Understand
The Palatina Art Collection

The gallery's highlights are found in a series of reception chambers dating from the Napoleonic period and decorated in the neoclassical style.

In the **Sala di Prometeo** is Fra' Filippo Lippi's *Madonna and Child with Stories from the Life of St Anne* (aka the Tondo Bartolini; 1452–53), one of the artist's major works. In the same room, admire the sombre *Madonna with Child and a Young St John the Baptist* (c 1490–95) by Botticelli. Its subject and execution stand in stark contrast to his earlier, often hedonistic, works – probably because it was painted after the death of Lorenzo the Magnificent, Botticelli's great patron, and during the ascendancy of the fire-and-brimstone preacher, Savonarola.

Madonna of the Window, named for the cloth-covered window in its background, is a charming work by Raphael, painted in 1513–14 towards the end of his glittering artistic career. Track the painting down in the **Sala di Ulisse**, once the bedroom of the Grand Dukes of Tuscany.

The gallery's sentimental favourite is undoubtedly Caravaggio's *Sleeping Cupid,* painted in 1608 in Malta, where the painter had fled after killing a man in a brawl and being exiled from Rome as a consequence. Find it in the **Sala dell'Educazione di Giove**.

The handsome **Sala dell'Iliade** showcases Raphael's *Portrait of a Woman* (aka *La Gravida*; c 1505–06) and the **Sala di Saturno** is home to his *Madonna with Child* and *St John the Baptist* (aka *The Madonna of the Chair*; 1511). Raphael's *Lady with a Veil* (aka *La Velata*; c 1516) holds court in the **Sala di Giove**.

The Venetian painter Titian (c 1490–1576) was a master of the portrait, and his painting of an unknown man (*Ritratto Virile*; c 1540–45) is one of his best. Known as *Portrait of a Man*, the subject displays a particularly piercing gaze. It's one of a number of Titians in the **Sala di Apollo**.

Giardino di Boboli

Giardino di Boboli

Behind Palazzo Pitti, the Boboli Gardens were laid out in the mid-16th century to a design by architect Niccolò Pericoli. At the upper, southern limit, beyond the box-hedged rose garden, beautiful views over the Florentine countryside unfold. In spring 2017, much to the joy of many a local Florentine who can be found promenading in Boboli on a Sunday afternoon, Florence's homegrown fashion house Gucci pledged €2 million to restore the gardens and their treasure trove of statues and fountains to their former pristine glory.

Museo delle Porcellane

Inside the 18th-century Palazzina del Cavaliere in the Boboli Gardens, this small museum houses an exquisite collection of European porcelain. Many pieces were brought to Florence from historic palaces in Parma, Piacenza and Sala Baganza in the late 19th century to decorate the Savoy family's Florentine residences.

Grotta del Buontalenti

Within the lower reaches of the gardens, don't miss this fantastical shell- and gem-encrusted *grotta,* a decorative grotto built by Bernardo Buontalenti between 1583 and 1593 for Francesco I de' Medici.

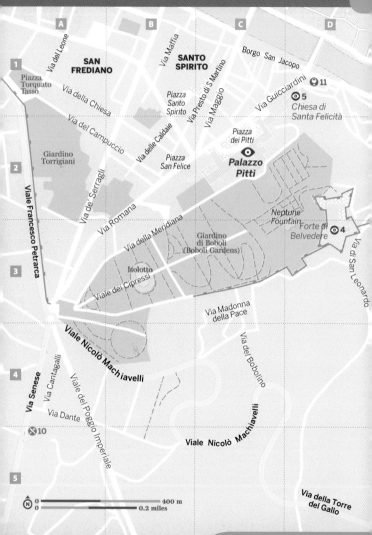

A
B
C
D

1

Via del Leone

SAN FREDIANO

Piazza Torquato Tasso

Via della Chiesa

Via del Campuccio

Via Maffia

SANTO SPIRITO

Piazza Santo Spirito

Via delle Caldaie

Via Presto S Martino

Via Maggio

Borgo San Jacopo

Via Guicciardini

☺11

◉5
Chiesa di Santa Felicità

Piazza dei Pitti

2

Giardino Torrigiani

Via de' Serragli

Piazza San Felice

Palazzo Pitti

Viale Francesco Petrarca

Via Romana

Via della Meridiana

Giardino di Boboli (Boboli Gardens)

Neptune Fountain

Forte di Belvedere ◉4

Via di San Leonardo

3

Isolotto

Viale dei Cipressi

Via Madonna della Pace

Via del Bobolino

4

Via Cantagalli

Viale Nicolò Machiavelli

Viale del Poggio Imperiale

Via Senese

Via Dante

⊗10

Viale Nicolò Machiavelli

5

0 ———— 400 m
0 ———— 0.2 miles

Via della Torre del Gallo

Corso dei Tintori

Via dei Molcontenti

Lungarno Generale Diaz

Via Tripoli

Piazza
Piave

Ponte
alle
Grazie

Arno

Lungarno Torrigiani

Via de' Bardi

Piazza
Nicola
Demidoff

Lungarno Serristori

Via dei Renai

Piazza de'
Mozzi

Via di San Niccolò

Piazza
Giuseppe
Poggi

Lungarno Benvenuto Cellini

Via dei Bastioni

Via della Fornace

Torre
San Niccolò

Giardino
dell'Iris

Giardino Bardini
(Bardini Gardens)

Villa e
Giardino
Bardini

Piazza
San Niccolò

Viale Giuseppe Poggi

Piazzale
Michelangelo

Via di Belvedere

Via Monte alle Croci

Via di San Miniato al Monte

**SAN
NICCOLÒ**

Via dell'Erta Canina

Via delle Porte Sante

**MONTE
ALLE
CROCI**

Viale Michelangelo

Basilica di
San Miniato
al Monte

Viale Galileo Galilei

Via Giramonte

Via Giramontino

Sights

Villa e Giardino Bardini

VILLA, GARDENS

1 Map p104, E2

This 17th-century villa and garden was named after 19th-century antiquarian art collector Stefano Bardini (1836–1922), who bought it in 1913 and restored its ornamental medieval garden. It has all the features of a quintessential Tuscan garden, including artificial grottos, orangery, marble statues and fountains. The villa houses two small museums: **Museo Pietro Annigoni**, with works by Italian painter Pietro Annigoni (1910–88), and **Museo Roberto Capucci**, showcasing Capucci-designed haute couture. End with city views from the romantic **roof terrace**. (☎055 263 85 99; www.bardini peyron.it; Costa San Giorgio 2, Via de' Bardi 1r; adult/reduced €8/6; ☉10am-7pm Tue-Sun)

Basilica di San Miniato al Monte

CHURCH

2 Map p104, G4

Five minutes' walk uphill from Piazzale Michelangelo is this wonderful Romanesque church, dedicated to St Minius, an early-Christian martyr in Florence said to have flown to this spot after his death down in the town (or, if you want to believe an alternative version, walked up the hill with his head tucked underneath his arm). The church dates from the early 11th century, although its typical Tuscan

Local Life

Piazzale Michelangelo

Turn your back on the bevy of ticky-tacky souvenir stalls flogging David statues and boxer shorts and take in the spectacular city panorama from this vast **square** (🚌13), pierced by one of Florence's two *David* copies. Sunset here is particularly dramatic. It's a 10-minute uphill walk along the serpentine road, paths and steps that scale the hillside from the Arno and Piazza Giuseppe Poggi; from Piazza San Niccolò walk uphill and bear left up the long flight of steps signposted Viale Michelangelo. Or take bus 13 from Stazione di Santa Maria Novella.

multicoloured marble facade was tacked on a couple of centuries later. (☎055 234 27 31; www.sanminiatoalmonte.it; Via Monte alle Croci; ☉9.30am-1pm & 3-8pm summer, to 7pm winter)

Torre San Niccolò

CITY GATE

3 Map p104, G2

Built in 1324, the best preserved of the city's medieval gates stands sentinel on the banks of the Arno. In summer, you can scale the steep stairs inside the tower with a guide to enjoy blockbuster river and city views. Visits are limited to 15 people at a time (no children under eight years), making advance reservations essential; book online, by email or by phone. Tours are cancelled when it rains. (☎055 276

82 24; http://musefirenze.it; Piazza Giuseppe Poggi; 30min guided visit €4; ⊙5-8pm daily 24 Jun-Sep)

Forte di Belvedere
FORTRESS

 Map p104, D3

Forte di Belvedere is a rambling fort designed by Bernardo Buontalenti for Grand Duke Ferdinando I at the end of the 16th century. From the massive bulwark, soldiers kept watch on four fronts – as much for internal security as to protect the Palazzo Pitti against foreign attack. Today, the fort hosts seasonal art exhibitions, which are well worth a peek if only to revel in the sweeping city panorama that can be had from the fort. Outside of exhibition times, the fort is closed. (www.museicivicifiorentini.comune.fi.it; Via di San Leonardo 1; free; ⊙hours vary)

Chiesa di Santa Felicità
CHURCH

 Map p104, D1

Possibly founded by Syrian merchants as early as the 2nd century, the current church is largely a Renaissance construction. Its most extraordinary feature is Brunelleschi's small Cappella Barbadori, which is adorned with frescoes by Jacopo Pontormo (1494–1557) of the *Annunciation* and a *Deposition from the Cross,* in garish reds, pinks and oranges. Note also that the Corridoio Vasariano passes right across the facade so the Medici could hear Mass like any good Christians, but without having to mix with

Basilica di San Miniato al Monte

the common folk. (Piazza di Santa Felicità; ⊙9.30am-noon & 3.30-5.30pm Mon-Sat)

Eating

La Leggenda dei Frati
TUSCAN €€€

6 ✕ Map p104, E2

Summertime's hottest address. At home in the grounds of historic Villa Bardini, Michelin-starred Legend of Friars enjoys the most romantic terrace with a view in Florence. Veggies are plucked fresh from the vegetable patch, tucked between waterfalls and ornamental beds in Giardino Bardini, and contemporary art jazzes up the classically chic interior. Cuisine is Tuscan, gastronomic and well worth the vital advance reservation. (☑055 068 05 45; www.laleggendadeifrati.it; Villa Bardini, Costa di San Giorgio 6a; menus €60 & €75, meals €70; ⊙12.30-2pm & 7.30-10pm Tue-Sun; 🛜)

La Bottega del Buon Caffè

TUSCAN €€€

 7 Map p104, G2

Farm to table is the philosophy of this Michelin-starred restaurant where head chef Antonello Sardi mesmerises diners from the stunning open kitchen. Veg and herbs arrive from the restaurant's own farm, Borgo Santo Pietro, in the Sienese hills. Breads and focaccia (the nut version is heavenly) are homemade and the olive oil used (special production from Vinci) is clearly only the best. (☑055 553 56 77; www.borgointhecity.com; Lungarno Benvenuto Cellini 69r; meals from €55; ⊙12.30-3pm Tue-Sat, 7.30-10.30pm Mon-Sat)

San Niccolò 39

SEAFOOD €€

8 Map p104, F2

With a street terrace at the front and hidden summer garden out the back, this contemporary address in quaint San Niccolò is a gem. Fish – both raw and cooked – is the house speciality, with chef Vanni cooking up a storm with his creative salted-cod burgers, swordfish steak with radicchio, and famous *linguine* (fat spaghetti) with squid ink and Cetara anchovy oil.

(☑055 200 13 97; www.sanniccolo39.com; Via di San Niccolò 39; meals €40; ⊙7-10.30pm Tue, 12.30-2.30pm & 7-10.30pm Wed-Sat; 🛜)

ZEB

TUSCAN €€

 9 Map p104, F2

Local gastronomes adore this modern, minimalist address with five-star wine list at the foot of the hill leading up to Piazzale Michelangelo, in village-like San Niccolò. Post-panorama, sit around the deli-style counter and indulge in a delicious choice of cold cuts and creative Tuscan dishes prepared by passionate chef Alberto Navari and his *mamma* Giuseppina. (☑055 234 28 64; www.zebgastronomia.com; Via San Miniato 2r; meals €35; ⊙12.30-3pm & 7.30-10.30pm Thu-Tue, closed Mon-Wed winter)

Da Ruggero

TUSCAN €€

10 Map p104, A5

A 10-minute stroll through Boboli Gardens (or along the street from Porta Romana) uncovers this trattoria, run by the gracious Corsi family since 1981 and much-loved for its pure, unadulterated Florentine tradition. Cuisine is Tuscan simple and hearty – *zuppa*

Local Life
Summer Hang-out

The enormous car-free, paved terrace fronting Palazzo Pitti is the hot spot in warm weather to lounge on the ground and chill with friends; sunset colours the entire vast facade of Palazzo Pitti a dazzling pink.

di ortiche (nettle soup), *spaghetti alla carrettiera* (spaghetti in a chilli-fired tomato sauce) and, of course, the iconic *bistecca* (T-bone steak). (📞 055 22 05 42; Via Senese 89r; meals €25; 🕑noon-2.30pm & 7-10.30pm Thu-Mon, closed mid-Jul–mid-Aug)

Drinking

Le Volpi e l'Uva   WINE BAR

11   Map p104, D1

This unassuming wine bar, hidden away by Chiesa di Santa Felicità, remains as appealing as the day it opened over a decade ago. Its food and wine pairings are first class – taste and buy boutique wines by small producers from all over Italy, matched perfectly with cheeses, cold meats and the best crostini in town. Wine-tasting classes too. (📞 055 239 81 32; www.levolpieluva.com; Piazza dei Rossi 1; 🕑11am-9pm Mon-Sat)

La Loggia   CAFE, RISTORANTE

12   Map p104, G3

With one of Florence's finest terraces overlooking the city from its hilltop perch, this historic cafe is predictably prime real estate. At home in an elegant 19th-century lodge once intended to house the sculptures of local lad Michelangelo, La Loggia serves drinks and light snacks beneath its vintage stone arches and classic Tuscan cuisine in its upmarket restaurant (meals €50). (📞 055 234

 Top Tip

Summer Clubbing

The hottest and hippest place to be seen in the city on hot sultry summer nights is **Flò** (Map p104, G2; 📞 055 65 07 91; www.flofirenze.com; Piazzale Michelangelo 84; 🕑7.30pm-4am summer), a truly ab fab seasonal lounge bar that pops up each May or June on Piazzale Michelangelo. There are different themed lounge areas, a dance floor and a VIP area (where you have no chance of reserving a table unless you're in the Florentine in-crowd).

28 32; http://ristorantelaloggia.it; Piazzale Michelangelo 1; 🕑11am-11pm; 🛜)

Surf Ventura   COCKTAIL BAR

13   Map p104, H2

If half a scooped-out papaya filled with alcohol is your cup of tea or you have an urge for a 100% bespoke cocktail made especially for you, hit this underground cocktail club. You'll need to fill in a membership form to get in, but one sip of a wacky cocktail dreamt up by the expert mixologists here and you won't regret it. (📞 055 68 85 89; Via Ser Ventura Monachi 21r; 🕑9.30pm-2am Wed-Mon)

Zoé   BAR

14   Map p104, F2

This savvy Oltrarno bar knows exactly what its hip punters want – a relaxed, faintly industrial space to hang out in all hours (well, almost). Be it breakfast, lunch, cocktails or after-dinner party, Zoé is your gal. Come springtime's warmth, the scene spills out onto a wooden decked street terrace out the front. Watch for DJs spinning tunes and parties; check its Facebook page. (☑055 24 31 11; www.facebook.com/zoebarfirenze; Via dei Renai 13r; ◷8.30am-3am; 🛜)

Shopping

Lorenzo Villoresi

PERFUME

15 🔒 Map p104, E2

Artisan perfumes, bodycare products, scented candles and stones, essential oils and room fragrances crafted by Florentine perfumer Lorenzo Villoresi meld distinctively Tuscan elements such as laurel, olive, cypress and iris with essential oils and essences from around the world. His bespoke fragrances are highly sought after and visiting his elegant boutique, at home in his family's 15th-century *palazzo*, is quite an experience. (☑055 234 11 87; www.lorenzovilloresi.it; Via de' Bardi 14; ◷10am-7pm Mon-Sat)

Antica Bottega Degli Orafi

JEWELLERY

16 🔒 Map p104, F2

Duck into this old-fashioned atelier to watch revered Florentine goldsmith Marco Baroni at work. Using all types of gold as well as iron, he crafts exquisite rings, bracelets, pendants

---

Understand

Clet

Should you notice something gone awry with street signs in Oltrarno – on a No Entry sign, a tiny black figure stealthily sneaking away with the white bar for example – you can be sure it is the work of French-born Clet Abraham, one of Florence's most popular street artists. In his Oltrarno **studio** (www.facebook.com/CLET-108974755823172; Via dell'Olmo 8r; ◷hours vary) you can buy stickers and postcards featuring his hacked traffic signs and, if you're lucky, catch a glimpse of the rebellious artist at work.

In 2011 Clet created quite a stir in his adopted city by installing, in the black of night, a life-sized figurine entitled *Uomo Comune* (*Common Man*) on Ponte alle Grazie (to which the city authorities turned a blind eye for a week before removing it). Should you fall completely and utterly head over heels in love with Clet's work, you can either order a reproduction street sign directly from his workshop (from €500) or purchase an original (numbered and signed, from €2500) limited edition from Mio Concept (p59) – Clet produces only 13 of each design.

Crafting a ring at Antica Bottega Degli Orafi

and earrings embedded with rare, precious and semi-precious gems and stones. His attention to detail – all his pieces feature intricate engraving – is remarkable. (☑ 055 246 90 32; www.marcobaronifirenze.com; Via dei Renai 3; ⏰ 9.30am-1pm & 3.30-7pm)

Legatoria Il Torchio

ARTS & CRAFTS

17 🔒 Map p104, E2

Peek into Erin Ciulla's cosy workshop for an insight into her contemporary approach to the traditional Florentine art of bookbinding. Inside you'll find a treasure trove of gifts, including hand-sewn leather books, marbled-paper photo frames and journals in the shape of musical instruments. Order in advance of your visit and she'll make a personalised item to your specifications. (☑ 05 5234 2862; www.legatoriailtorchio.com; Via de' Bardi 17; ⏰ 10am-1.30pm & 2.30-7pm Mon-Fri, 10am-1pm Sat)

Explore

Oltrarno

Literally the 'other side of the Arno', this atmospheric neighbourhood is the traditional home of the city's artisans and its streets are peppered with *botteghe* (workshops), designer boutiques and hybrid forms of both. Food and drink is also a strength – prepared using artisanal ingredients, of course – and there's an ever-growing number of fashionable restaurants and bars to lure you across the river.

The Sights in a Day

☀ Explore the area around **Basilica di Santo Spirito** (p118), visiting the Brunelleschi-designed church and local *botteghe* to watch artisans at work. Break mid-morning for a smoothie or turbo-boosting aloe vera shot at **Raw** (p120).

☀ Lunch on traditional Tuscan cuisine at **Il Santo Bevitore** (p119), a bespoke *panino* (sandwich) at **S.Forno** (p121) or a salad at organic **Carduccio** (p120). Later admire Masaccio's frescoes in **Cappella Brancacci** (p118). With an advance reservation, a delightful afternoon can be spent exploring the romantic, 19th-century walled garden of **Giardino Torrigiani** (p120). Otherwise, delve into the art galleries and boutiques peppering the increasingly trendy 'hood of **San Frediano**, **Via di Santo Spirito** and **Borgo San Jacopo**.

☾ Enjoy evening drinks and gourmet snacks at **Il Santino** (p123), moving to **Il Santo Bevitore** (p119) for a candlelit dinner. Or start with cocktails at **Mad Souls & Spirits** (p123), followed by sensational modern Tuscan cuisine at **Essenziale** (p119). End with live music at **La Cité** (p124), spaghetti jazz at **Santarosa Bistrot** (p122) or late-night drinks at 'secret' speakeasy **Rasputin** (p123).

For a local's day in Oltrarno, see p114.

Local Life
City of Artisans (p114)

Best of Florence

Getting There

🚶 **Walk** From Piazza della Stazione walk southeast to the Duomo. From Via Roma, cross the Ponte Vecchio and you're in Oltrarno.

Local Life
City of Artisans

In our factory-made world, the old-fashioned *botteghe* of the Oltrarno are a particular delight. Florence's famed guilds may now be defunct, but many local artisans – welders and goldsmiths, framers and bookbinders, shoemakers and seamstresses – still hand down their craft from generation to generation on this side of the Arno.

❶ A Bookbinding Legend

The quaint old shopfront of **Giulio Giannini e Figlio** (☎055 21 26 21; www.giuliogiannini.it; Piazza dei Pitti 37r; ⏲10am-7pm Mon-Sat, 11am-6.30pm Sun) has watched Palazzo Pitti turn pink with the evening sun since 1856. One of Florence's oldest artisan families, the Giannini – bookbinders by trade – make and sell marbled paper, beautifully bound books, stationery and so on. Don't miss the workshop upstairs.

2 Fashionable Leather

The Tattanelli family business started in 1945 with quality leather bags, wallets and attache cases, but branched out into leather clothing in 1971 when this boutique, **Casini Firenze** (📞055 21 93 24; www.casinifirenze.it; Piazza dei Pitti 30-31r; 🕙10am-7pm Mon-Sat, 11am-6pm Sun), first opened. Shop here for stylish men's and women's bags, shoes, belts and ready-to-wear clothing.

3 Contemporary Book-Sculpting

Every book tells a different story in this absolutely fascinating artist's workshop, home to Milan-born **Lorenzo Perrone** (📞340 274402; www.libribianchi.info; Borgo Tegolaio 59r; 🕙hours vary) who creates snow-white *libri bianchi* (White Books) – aka sublime book sculptures – out of plaster, glue, acrylic and various upcycled objects. His working hours are, somewhat predictably, erratic; call ahead.

4 Meet a Jeweller

Once a mechanic's shop, **Officine Nora** (www.officinenora.it; Via dei Preti 2-4; 🕙11am-1pm & 3.30-7.30pm Mon-Fri) is a seriously cool work space for contemporary jewellery-makers, bringing Florence's rich history of expert goldsmithing right up to date. Watch resident artists at work in the luminous loft – much of the dazzling wearable art is for sale. To ensure a warm welcome, email or call in advance.

5 A Calligrapher & Company

&Co (And Company; 📞055 21 99 73; www. andcompanyshop.com; Via Maggio 51r; 🕙10.30am-1pm & 3-7pm Mon-Sat) – a Pandora's box of beautiful objects – is the love child of Florence-born, British-raised callligrapher and graphic designer Betty Soldi and her vintage-loving husband, Matteo Perduca. Their extraordinary boutique showcases Betty's customised cards, decorative paper products, upcycled homewares and custom fragrances alongside work by other designers.

6 Shoes from Francesco

Hand-stitched leather is the cornerstone of **Francesco** (Via di Santo Spirito 62r; 🕙10am-1pm & 3.30-7.30pm Mon-Sat, 10am-1pm Sun, closed 2 weeks Aug), a tiny family business with an enchantingly old-fashioned workshop off Piazza di Santo Spirito. Come here for silk-soft, ready-to-wear and made-to-measure men's and women's shoes.

7 Traditional Florentine Fabrics

Master weavers at **Antico Setificio Fiorentino** (📞055 21 38 61; www. anticosetificiofiorentino.com; Via L Bartolini 4; 🕙by apppintment only 10am-6pm Mon-Fri) produce traditional Florentine fabrics, brocades and damasks on 12 looms: six hand-looms from the 18th century and six semi-mechanical looms from the 19th century. Head here to buy fabric or to browse accessories made from hand-woven silk.

A Lungarno di Santa Rosa **B** Ponte Amerigo Vespucci **C** **D**

1 15

Piazza di Verzaia

Via Sant' Onofrio

Lungarno Soderini

Piazza di Cestello

Borgo San Frediano

2 Viale Lodovico Ariosto

10

Piazza dei Nerli

4

16 20

Borgo San Frediano

Via San Giovanni

Via del Drago d'Oro

Via del Leone

SAN FREDIANO

Via dell'Orto

6

Borgo della Stella

Via di Camaldoli

Piazza Piattellina

Piazza del Carmine

22

3

1

Cappella Brancacci

Via Santa Monaca

Via del Leone

11

Viale Francesco Petrarca

Piazza Torquato Tasso

Via dell'Ardiglione

Via de' Serragli

Via Maffia

4 Via della Chiesa

Via del Campuccio

Via della Chiesa

For reviews see	
Sights	p118
Eating	p119
Drinking	p122
Shopping	p125

Giardino Torrigiani

Via del Campuccio

5 N 0 / 0   200 m / 0.1 miles

E

F

G

H

1

Via della Vigna Nuova

Lungarno Amerigo Vespucci

Via del Parione

Via de' Tornabuoni

2

Ponte alla Carraia

Lungarno Corsini

Arno

Piazza Santa Trinita

Borgo SS Apostoli

Piazza N Sauro
13

5

18

Via de' Geppi

Via di Santo Spirito

Ponte Santa Trinita

Lungarno degli Acciaiuoli

3

Via Maffia

SANTO SPIRITO

Via de' Coverelli

Piazza de' Frescobaldi

Palazzo Frescobaldi

Borgo San Jacopo
23

Via Presto di S. Martino

Via dello Sprone

24

Piazza della Passera

Via de' Ramaglianti

Via de' Barbadori

Via de' Bardi

4

Fondazione Salvatore Romano
2

Basilica di Santo Spirito
3

Via de' Michelozzi

Via de' Vellutini

Via dei Velluti

Via Sguazza

Via Toscanella

19

Piazza Santo Spirito

14

21

12

17

9

Via Sant'Agostino

7

Sdrucciolo de Pitti

8

Via delle Caldaie

Via Mazzetta

Via Maggio

Piazza dei Pitti

5

Piazza San Felice

Giardino di Boboli (Boboli Gardens)

Sights

Cappella Brancacci
CHAPEL

1 Map p116, C3

Fire in the 18th century practically destroyed 13th-century **Basilica di Santa Maria del Carmine** (Piazza del Carmine), but it spared the magnificent frescoes in this chapel – a treasure of paintings by Masolino da Panicale, Masaccio and Filippino Lippi commissioned by rich merchant Felice Brancacci upon his return from Egypt in 1423. The chapel entrance is to the right of the main church entrance. Only 30 people can visit at a time, limited to 30 minutes in high season; tickets include admission to the Fondazione Salvatore Romano. (📞055 238 21 95; http://museicivicifiorentini. comune.fi.it; Piazza del Carmine 14; adult/ reduced €6/4.50; 🕙10am-5pm Wed-Sat & Mon, 1-5pm Sun)

Fondazione Salvatore Romano
MUSEUM

2 Map p116, E4

For a change of pace from the Renaissance, head to this Gothic-style former refectory safeguarding an imposing wall fresco by Andrea Orcagna depicting the *Last Supper and the Crucifixion* (c 1370), one of the largest 14th-century paintings to survive. The museum itself displays a collection of rare 11th-century Romanesque sculpture, paintings and antique furniture donated to the city by art collector

and antiquarian Salvatore Romano (1875–1955). Tickets can only be bought at nearby Cappella Brancacci; the same ticket covers admission to both sights. (Cenacolo di Santo Spirito; 📞055 28 70 43; http://museicivicifiorentini. comune.fi.it; Piazza Santo Spirito 29; adult/ reduced €7/5; 🕙10am-4pm Sat-Mon)

Basilica di Santo Spirito
CHURCH

3 Map p116, F4

The facade of this Brunelleschi church, smart on Florence's most shabby-chic piazza, makes a striking backdrop to open-air concerts in summer. Inside, the basilica's length is lined with 38 semicircular chapels (covered with a plain wall in the 1960s), and a colonnade of grey *pietra forte* Corinthian columns injects monumental grandeur. Artworks to look for include Domenico di Zanobi's *Madonna of the Relief* (1485) in the Cappella Velutti, in which the Madonna wards off a little red devil with a club. (Piazza Santo Spirito; 🕙9.30am-12.30pm & 4-5.30pm Thu-Tue)

☑ Top Tip

Summer Concerts

Watch for open-air concerts, film screenings and other edgy, summertime cultural happenings on Piazza Santo Spirito.

Eating

Essenziale
TUSCAN €€

4 Map p116, C2

There's no finer showcase for modern Tuscan cuisine than this loft-style restaurant in a 19th-century warehouse. Preparing dishes at the kitchen bar, in rolled-up shirt sleeves and navy butcher's apron, is dazzling young chef Simone Cipriani. Order one of his tasting menus to sample the full range of his inventive, thoroughly modern cuisine inspired by classic Tuscan dishes. (055 247 69 56; http://essenziale. me/; Piazza di Cestello 3r; 3-/5-/7-course tasting menu €35/55/75, brunch €28; 7-10pm Tue-Sat, 11am-4pm Sun;)

Il Santo Bevitore
TUSCAN €€

5 Map p116, E3

Reserve or arrive right on 7.30pm to snag the last table at this ever-popular address, an ode to stylish dining where gastronomes eat by candlelight in a vaulted, whitewashed, bottle-lined interior. The menu is a creative reinvention of seasonal classics: risotto with monkfish, red turnip and fennel; *ribollita* (bean, vegetable and bread soup) with kale; or chicken liver terrine with brioche and a Vin Santo reduction. (055 21 12 64; www.ilsanto bevitore.com; Via di Santo Spirito 64-66r; meals €40; 12.30-2.30pm & 7.30-11.30pm, closed Sun lunch & Aug)

PHOTOGOLFER/SHUTTERSTOCK ©

Cappella Brancacci

Burro e Acciughe

TUSCAN €€

6 Map p116, B3

Carefully sourced, quality ingredients drive this fishy newcomer that woos punters with a short but stylish choice of raw (tartare and carpaccio) and cooked fish dishes. The gnocchi topped with octopus *ragù* (stew) is out of this world, as is the *baccalà* (salted cod) with creamed leeks, turnip and deep-fried polenta wedges. Excellent wine list too. (Butter & Anchovies; ☑055 045 72 86; www.burroeacciughe.com; Via dell'Orto 35; meals €35; ⏱noon-2pm & 7pm-midnight Fri-Sun, 7pm-midnight Tue-Thu)

Raw

HEALTH FOOD €

7 Map p116, E4

Be it a turmeric, ginger or aloe vera shot or a gently warmed, raw vegan burger served on a stylish slate-and-wood platter, Raw hits the spot. Everything served here is freshly made and raw – to sensational effect. Herbs are grown in the biodynamic greenhouse of charismatic and hugely knowledgeable chef Caroline, a Swedish architect before moving to Florence. (☑055 21 93 79; Via Sant' Agostino 9; meals €7.50; ⏱11am-4pm & 7-10pm Thu & Fri, 11am-4pm Sat, Sun, Tue & Wed; 🛜)

Gurdulù

RISTORANTE €€

8 Map p116, E5

Gourmet Gurdulù seduces fashionable Florentines with razor-sharp interior design, magnificent craft cocktails and seasonal market cuisine with a hint of Balkan spice by Albanian female chef Entiana Osmenzeza. A hybrid drink-dine, this address is as much about noshing gourmet *aperitivi* (pre-dinner drinks) snacks over expertly mixed cocktails – thanks to talented female mixologist Sabrina Galloni – as it is about dining exceedingly well. (☑055 28 22 23; www.gurdulu.com; Via delle Caldaie 12r; meals €40, tasting menu €55; ⏱7.30-11pm Tue-Sat, 12.30-2.30pm & 7.30-11pm Sun; 🛜)

Carduccio

ORGANIC €

9 Map p116, F4

With just a handful of tables inside and a couple more alfresco, this

Local Life
A Secret Garden

Vast secret **Giardino Torrigiani** (Map p116, D4; ☑055 22 45 27; www.giardinotorrigiani.it; Via de' Serragli 144; 1½hr guided tours by donation; ⏱advance reservation via email) is Europe's largest privately owned green space within a historic centre and can be visited with the charismatic Marquis Vanni Torrigiani Malaspina and his wife, Susanna.

Designed during the Romantic movement in the early 19th century, the garden frames the original 16th-century villa and later 19th-century house. Admire rare tree species, a beautifully restored greenhouse and city walls built under Cosimo I in 1544 (one of six sets of walls to be built around Florence at different times).

salotto bio (organic living room) oozes intimacy. Miniature cabbage 'flowers' decorate each table, fruit and veg crates stack up by the bar, and the menu is 100% organic. Knock back a ginger and turmeric shot (€3) or linger over delicious salads, soups, vegan burgers or pumpkin and leek patties. (☑055 238 20 70; www.carduccio.com; Sdrucciolo de Pitti 10r; meals €15; ☺8am-8pm Mon-Sat, 10am-5pm Sun; 🛜)

iO Osteria Personale   TUSCAN €€€

10 Map p116, A2

Persuade everyone at your table to order the tasting menu to avoid the torture of picking just one dish – everything on the menu at this fabulously contemporary and creative *osteria* (casual tavern) is to die for. Pontedera-born chef Nicolò Baretti uses only seasonal products, natural ingredients and traditional flavours – to sensational effect. (☑055 933 13 41; www.io-osteriapersonale.it; Borgo San Frediano 167r; 4-/5-/6-course tasting menus €40/48/55; ☺7.30-10pm Mon-Sat)

S.Forno   BAKERY €

11 Map p116, D4

Shop at this hipster bakery, around for at least a century, for fresh breads and pastries baked to sweet perfection in its ancient *forno* (oven). Gourmet dried products stack up on vintage shelves and local baker Angelo cooks up soups, quiches and bespoke *panini* (€4 to €6) too, to eat in or out. (☑055 239 85 80; Via

Local Life
Piazza della Passera

This bijou square with no passing traffic is a gourmet gem. Pick from cheap wholesome tripe in various guises at **Il Magazzino** (Map p116, G4; ☑055 21 59 69; www.tripperiailmagazzino.com; Piazza della Passera 2/3; meals €30; ☺noon-3pm & 7.30-11pm); vegetarian at **5 e Cinque** (☑055 274 15 83; Piazza della Passera 1; meals €25; ☺noon-3pm & 7.30-10pm Tue-Sun; 🛜🌿); or upmarket Tuscan classics at veteran address **Trattoria 4 Leoni** (Map p116, G4; ☑055 21 85 62; www.4leoni.com; Piazza della Passera 2/3; meals €45; ☺noon-midnight), known for its brilliantly blue *bistecca alla fiorentina* (chargrilled T-bone steak) cooked up since 1550.

Santa Monaco 3r; ☺7.30am-7.30pm Mon-Fri, from 8am Sat & Sun)

Tamerò   ITALIAN €€

12 Map p116, E4

A happening pasta bar on Florence's hippest square: admire chefs at work in the open kitchen while you wait for a table. A buoyant, party-loving crowd flocks here to fill up on imaginative fresh pasta, giant salads and copious cheese and salami platters. Decor is trendy industrial, *aperitivo* 'happy hour' (€9) is 6.30pm to 9pm, and weekend DJs spin sets from 10pm. (☑055 28 25 96; www.tamero.it; Piazza Santo Spirito 11r; meals €25; ☺noon-3pm & 6.30pm-2am Tue-Sun; 🛜)

Understand
Ponte Vecchio

Dating to 1345, Ponte Vecchio was the only Florentine bridge to survive destruction at the hands of retreating German forces in 1944. Above the jewellers' shops on the eastern side, the Corridoio Vasariano (Vasari Corridor) is a 16th-century passageway between the Uffizi and Palazzo Pitti that runs around, rather than through, the medieval Torre dei Mannelli at the bridge's southern end. The first documentation of a stone bridge here, at the narrowest crossing point along the entire length of the Arno, dates from 972.

Floods in 1177 and 1333 destroyed the bridge, and in 1966 it came close to being destroyed again. Many of the jewellers with shops on the bridge were convinced the floodwaters would sweep away their livelihoods; fortunately, the bridge held.

They're still here. Indeed, the bridge has twinkled with the glittering wares of jewellers, their trade often passed down from generation to generation, ever since the 16th century, when Ferdinando I de' Medici ordered them here to replace the often malodorous presence of the town butchers, who used to toss unwanted leftovers into the river.

Gelateria La Carraia   GELATO €

13   Map p116, E2

One glance at the constant line out the door of this bright green-and-citrus shop with exciting flavours (ricotta and pear, English soup, the best mint in town) and you'll know you're at a Florentine favourite. (☎055 28 06 95; Piazza Nazario Sauro 25r; cones & tubs €1.50-6; ☺10.30am-midnight summer, 11am-10pm winter)

Gustapanino   SANDWICHES €

14   Map p116, E4

It's dead simple to spot what many Florentines rate as the city's best *eno-paninoteca* (hip wine and sandwich stop), with no seating but bags of

square space and church steps outside – just look for the long line in front. (www.facebook.com/pages/Gustapanino; Piazza Santo Spirito; focacce from €3.50; ☺11am-8pm Mon-Sat, noon-5pm Sun)

Drinking

Santarosa Bistrot   BAR

15   Map p116, A1

The living is easy at this hipster garden bistro-bar, snug against a chunk of ancient city wall in the flowery Santarosa gardens. Comfy cushioned sofas built from recycled wooden crates sit beneath trees alfresco; food is superb (meals €30); and mixologists behind the bar complement an excellent wine list curated by Enoteca Pitti Gola e Cantina (p123) with serious craft cocktails. (☎055 230 90 57; www.facebook.com/santarosa.bistrot; Lungarno di Santarosa; ⊗8am-midnight; ☎)

Mad Souls & Spirits COCKTAIL BAR

16 Map p116, D2

At this bar of the moment, cult alchemists Neri Fantechi and Julian Biondi woo a discerning fashionable crowd with their expertly crafted cocktails, served in a tiny aqua-green and red-brick space that couldn't be more spartan. A potted cactus decorates each scrubbed wood table and the humorous cocktail menu is the height of irreverence. Check the 'Daily Madness' blackboard for wild 'n' wacky specials. (☎055 627 16 21; www.facebook.com/madsoulsandspirits; Borgo San Frediano 38r; ⊗6pm-2am Thu-Sun, to midnight Mon & Wed; ☎)

Rasputin COCKTAIL BAR

17 Map p116, F4

The 'secret' speakeasy everyone knows about, it has no sign outside: disguised as a chapel of sorts, look for the tiny entrance with two-seat wooden pew, crucifix on the wall, vintage pics and tea lights flickering in the doorway. Inside, it's back to the 1930s with period furnishings, an exclusive vibe and barmen mixing Prohibition-era cocktails. Reservations (phone or Facebook page) recommended. (☎055 28 03 99; www.facebook.com/rasputinfirenze; Borgo Tegolaio 21r; ⊗8pm-2am)

 Local Life
Wine Tasting

If you're in Tuscany for the wine, an evening of tastings over dinner with expert and incredibly entertaining sommeliers Edoardo, Manuele and Zeno at **Enoteca Pitti Gola e Cantina** (☎055 21 27 04; www.pittigolae cantina.com; Piazza dei Pitti 16; ⊗1pm-midnight Wed-Mon) is an essential. Floor-to-ceiling shelves of expertly curated, small-production Tuscan and Italian wines fill the tiny bar and casual dining (excellent cured meats, homemade pasta) is around a handful of marble-topped tables.

Exceptional wine tastings range from simple wine flights (three wines €20) to lunch tastings (four wines with lunch €35) and a full-blown evening of tastings over dinner (15 to 20 wines €160, weekends only). Reservations are essential. The team has its own fully fledged restaurant with predictably exceptional wine list, **Osteria dell'Enoteca** (☎055 21 27 04; www.osteriadellenoteca.com; Via Romana 70r; meals €30; ⊗noon-2.30pm & 7-11pm Wed-Mon), nearby.

Il Santino WINE BAR

18 Map p116, E3

Kid sister to top-notch restaurant Il Santo Bevitore two doors down the street, this intimate wine bar with exposed stone walls and marble bar is a stylish spot for pairing cured meats, cheeses and Tuscan staples with a

Local Life

Cocktail Culture

There is no finer neighbourhood for hobnobbing with fashionable Florentines over craft cocktails than trendy **San Frediano** in the Oltrarno; top spots include Mad Souls & Spirits (p123), 'secret' speakeasy Rasputin (p123) and Balkan-influenced Gurdulù (p120). For creative sake-based fusion cocktails in the company of Japanese tapas, head to smart Japanese cocktail bar **Kawaii** (📞055 28 14 00; www.ristorantemomoyama.it; Borgo San Frediano 8r; ⏰6pm-1am).

carefully curated selection of wine – many by local producers – and artisan beers. (📞055 230 28 20; Via di Santo Spirito 60r; ⏰12.30-11pm)

Ditta Artigianale

CAFE, BAR

 19 Map p116, G4

The second branch of Florence's premier coffee roaster and gin bar treats its faithful hipster clientele to full-blown dining in a 1950s-styled interior alongside its signature speciality coffees, gin cocktails and laid-back vibe. Think bright geometric-patterned wallpaper, comfy gold and pea-green armchairs, a mezzanine restaurant up top, buzzing ground-floor bar with great cocktails down below, and a tiny street terrace out the back. (📞055 045 71 63; www.dittaartigianale.it; Via dello Sprone 5r; ⏰8am-midnight Mon-Fri, 9am-midnight Sat & Sun; 📶)

La Cité

BAR

 20 Map p116, D2

A hip cafe-bookshop with an eclectic choice of vintage seating, La Cité makes a wonderful, intimate venue for book readings, after-work drinks and fantastic live music – jazz, swing, world music. Check its Facebook page for the week's events. (📞055 21 03 87; www.lacitelibreria.info; Borgo San Frediano 20r; ⏰2pm-2am Mon-Sat, 3pm-2am Sun; 📶)

Volume

BAR

21 Map p116, E4

Armchairs, recycled and upcycled vintage furniture, books to read, jukebox, crepes and a tasty choice of nibbles with coffee or a light lunch give this hybrid cafe-bar-gallery real appeal – all in an old hat-making workshop with tools and wooden moulds strewn around. Watch for various music, art and DJ events and other happenings. (📞055 238 14 60; www.volumefirenze.com; Piazza Santo Spirito 3r; ⏰8.30am-1.30am)

 Top Tip

Markets

Watch for an arts and crafts market on Piazza Santo Spirito on the second Sunday of each month, and an organic farmers market on the third Sunday. Most days, a handful of stalls selling fruit and veg pepper the lovely square.

Dolce Vita BAR

22 Map p116, D3

Going strong since the 1980s, this veteran bar with a distinct club vibe is an Oltrarno hot spot for after-work drinks, cocktails and DJ sets. Its chic, design-driven interior gets a new look every month thanks to constantly changing photography and contemporary art exhibitions. In summer, its decked terrace is the place to be seen (shades obligatory). Live bands, too. (☏055 28 45 95; www.dolcevitaflorence.com; Piazza del Carmine 6r; ⏰7pm-1.30am Sun-Wed, to 2am Thu-Sat, closed 2 weeks Aug)

Gustapanino (p122)

Shopping

Obsequium WINE

23 Map p116, G3

Tuscan wines, wine accessories and gourmet foods, including truffles, in one of the city's finest wine shops – on the ground floor of one of Florence's best-preserved medieval towers to boot. Not sure which wine to buy? Linger over a glass or indulge in a three-wine tasting with (€20 to €40) or without (€15 to €30) an accompanying *taglieri* (board) of mixed cheese and salami. (☏055 21 68 49; www.obsequium. it; Borgo San Jacopo 17/39; ⏰10am-10pm Mon, to 9pm Tue & Wed, to midnight Thu-Sat, noon-midnight Sun)

Byørk FASHION & ACCESSORIES

24 Map p116, G4

Cutting-edge fashion plus 'Zines, books, magazines' is what this trendy concept store, incongruously wedged between tatty old artisan workshops on an Oltrarno backstreet, sells. It is the creation of well-travelled Florentine and fashionista Filippo Anzaione, whose taste in Italian and other contemporary European designers is impeccable. (☏333 9795839; www. bjorkflorence.com; Via della Sprone 25r; ⏰2.30-7.30pm Mon, 10.30am-1.30pm & 2.30-7.30pm Tue-Sat)

Explore

Pisa

Once a maritime power to rival Genoa and Venice, Pisa now draws its fame from an architectural project gone terribly wrong. But the world-famous Leaning Tower is just one of many noteworthy sights in this compact and compelling city. Romanesque buildings, Gothic churches and Renaissance piazzas abound, and there's also a vibrant and affordable cafe and bar scene.

The Sights in a Day

To avoid leaving Pisa feeling oddly deflated by one of Europe's great landmarks, save the **Leaning Tower** (p129) and its oversized **square** (p128) for the latter part of the day. Upon arrival, indulge in peaceful meanderings along the Arno river, over its bridges and through Pisa's medieval heart. Over coffee, discover the last monumental wall **painting** (p134) Keith Haring did before he died, and enjoy art genius at **Museo Nazionale di San Matteo** (p133) and **Palazzo Blu** (p133).

Lunch with locals at **Sottobosco** (p135) or **Osteria Bernardo** (p134). Then hit Piazza dei Miracoli and Pisa's blockbuster sights. When the tourist throng gets too much, retreat to the leafy **Botanical Garden** (p133) for green peace or **Gelateria De' Coltelli** (p135) for sensational gelato riverside.

Return to the train station via handsome **Piazza dei Cavalieri** (pictured left) with its elegant *palazzi* (mansions) and bustling cafe-bar scene. Enjoy an *aperitivo* (pre-dinner drink with nibbles) here or continue to a bar on **Piazza delle Vettovaglie** or **Bazeel** (p135) to watch the sun set over the Arno.

Top Sight

Piazza dei Miracoli (p128)

Best of Pisa

Architecture
Piazza dei Miracoli (p128)

Views
Leaning Tower (p129)

Passeggiata
Orto e Museo Botanico (p133)

Getting There

Train Regular services leave Florence (€8.40, 1¼ hours) for Pisa Centrale station.

Car Take the toll-free SCG FI-PI-LI (SS67) from Florence. Street parking costs €2 per hour. Park outside the historic centre's Limited Traffic Zone (ZTL); find a free car park on Lungarno Guadalongo, south side of the Arno.

Top Sights
Piazza dei Miracoli

No Tuscan sight is more immortalised in kitsch souvenirs than the iconic tower teetering on the edge of this vast green square, also known as Piazza del Duomo (Cathedral Sq). Its lawns provide an urban carpet on which Europe's most extraordinary concentration of Romanesque buildings lounge: the *duomo* (cathedral), *battistero* (baptistry) and *campanile* (bell tower; aka the Leaning Tower).

Campo dei Miracoli

Map p132, B1

050 83 50 11

www.opapisa.it

Leaning Tower of Pisa

Leaning Tower

Yes, it's true: Pisa's famous **tower** (Torre Pendente; Map p132; ☎050 83 50 11; www.opapisa.it; Piazza dei Miracoli; €18; ⊗8am-8pm Apr-Sep, 9am-7pm Oct, to 6pm Mar, 10am-5pm Nov-Feb) really does lean. The steep climb up its 300-odd steps is strenuous and can be tricky (children under eight are not admitted; those aged eight to 12 years must hold an adult's hand), but the views from the top make it well worthwhile. Buy tickets from one of two well-signposted ticket offices: the main ticket office behind the tower or the smaller office inside Museo delle Sinopie (p130).

Duomo

Pisa's huge 11th-century **duomo** (Duomo di Santa Maria Assunta; Map p132; ☎050 83 50 11; www.opapisa.it; Piazza dei Miracoli; free; ⊗10am-8pm Apr-Sep, to 7pm Oct, to 6pm Nov-Mar), with its striking cladding of green and cream marble (a 13th-century addition), was the blueprint for Romanesque churches throughout Tuscany. The elliptical dome, the first of its kind in Europe at the time, dates from 1380 and the wooden ceiling decorated with 24-carat gold is a legacy of Medici rule.

Battistero

Construction of the cupcake-style **Battistero** (Battistero di San Giovanni; Map p132; ☎050 83 50 11; www.opapisa.it; Piazza dei Miracoli; €5, combination ticket with Camposanto or Museo delle Sinopie €7, Camposanto & Museo €8; ⊗8am-8pm Apr-Sep, 9am-7pm Oct, to 6pm Mar, 10am-5pm Nov-Feb) began in 1152, but the building was remodelled and continued by Nicola and Giovanni Pisano more than a century later and finally completed in the 14th century. Don't leave without climbing to the Upper Gallery to listen to the custodian demonstrate the double dome's remarkable acoustics and echo effects.

☑ Top Tips

▶ There are limited admissions to the Leaning Tower: book in advance online or grab the first available slot as soon as you arrive; ticket desks are behind the tower and in the Museo delle Sinopie.

▶ Admission to the *duomo* is free, but you need to show a ticket – either for one of the other sights or a *duomo* coupon distributed at ticket offices.

▶ From mid-June until late August or early September, the Leaning Tower and Camposanto stay open until 10pm (last admission 9.30pm).

✗ Take a Break

Pick up a *cecina* (chickpea pizza) or a *focaccine* (small flat roll) from Pizzeria Il Montino (p134).

Break with coffee or a drink at historic Caffè Pasticceria Salza (p135).

Inside the Battistero, a hexagonal marble pulpit (1260) by Nicola Pisano is the undoubted highlight. Inspired by the Roman sarcophagi in the Camposanto, Pisano used powerful classical models to enact scenes from biblical legend. His figure of Daniel, who supports one of the corners of the pulpit on his shoulders, is particularly extraordinary.

Camposanto

Soil shipped from Calvary during the Crusades is said to lie within the white walls of this hauntingly beautiful **cloistered quadrangle** (Map p132; ✆050 83 50 11; www.opapisa.it; Piazza dei Miracoli; €5, combination ticket with Battistero or Museo delle Sinopie €7, Battistero & Museo €8; ⊙8am-8pm Apr-Sep, 9am-7pm Oct, to 6pm Mar, 10am-5pm Nov-Feb) where prominent Pisans were once buried. Some of the sarcophagi here are of Graeco-Roman origin, recycled during the Middle Ages. During WWII, Allied artillery unfortunately destroyed many of the 14th- and 15th-century frescoes that once covered the cloister walls.

Museo delle Sinopie

This **museum** (Map p132; ✆050 83 50 11; www.opapisa.it; Piazza dei Miracoli; €5, combination ticket with Battistero or Camposanto €7, Battistero & Camposanto €8; ⊙8am-8pm Apr-Sep, 9am-7pm Oct, to 6pm Mar, 10am-5pm Nov-Feb) safeguards several *sinopie* (preliminary sketches) drawn by artists in red earth pigment on the walls of the Camposanto in the 14th and 15th centuries before frescoes were painted over them. It offers a compelling study in fresco painting technique, with short films and scale models filling in the gaps.

Understand
The Triumph of Death

Among the few of the Camposanto's frescoes to survive was this remarkable illustration of Hell (1333–41), attributed to Buonamico Buffalmacco. Fortunately, the mirrors once stuck next to the graphic images of the damned being roasted alive on spits have been removed – originally, viewers would have seen their own faces in the horrific scene.

Understand
Why It Leans

In 1160 Pisa boasted 10,000-odd towers, but no *campanile* (bell tower) for its cathedral. Loyal Pisan, Berta di Bernardo, righted this in 1172 when she died and left a legacy of 60 pieces of silver in her will to the city to get cracking on a *campanile*.

Ironically, when Bonnano Pisano set to work on the world's most famous *campanile* in 1173, he did not realise what shaky ground he was on: beneath Piazza dei Miracoli's lawns lay a treacherous mix of sand and clay, 40m deep. And when work stopped five years on, with just three storeys completed, Italy's stump of an icon already tilted. Building resumed in 1272, workers compensating for the lean by building straight up from the lower storeys to create a subtle banana curve. By the 19th century, many were convinced the tower was a mere whimsical folly of its inventors, built deliberately to lean.

In 1838 a clean-up job to remove muck oozing from the base of the tower exposed, once and for all, the true nature of its precarious foundations. In the 1950s the seven bells inside the tower, each sounding a different musical note and rung from the ground by 14 men since 1370, were silenced for fear of a catastrophic collapse. In 1990 the tower was closed to the public. Engineers placed 1000 tonnes of lead ingots on the north side to counteract the subsidence on the south side. Steel bands were wrapped around the 2nd storey to keep it together.

Then in 1995 the tower slipped a whole 2.5mm. Steel braces were slung around the 3rd storey of the tower and attached to heavy hydraulic A-frame anchors some way from the northern side. The frames were replaced by steel cables, attached to neighbouring buildings. The tower held in place, engineers gingerly removed 70 tonnes of earth from below the northern foundations, forcing the tower to sink to its 18th-century level – and correct the lean by 2011 to 43.8cm. Success...

Every year scientists carry out tests on Pisa's pearly white leaning tower to measure its lean and check that it's stable. Ironically, results in 2013 showed that the world's most famous leaning tower had, in fact, lost 2.5cm of its iconic lean, with some scientists even predicting a complete self-straightening by the year 2300. Let's hope not.

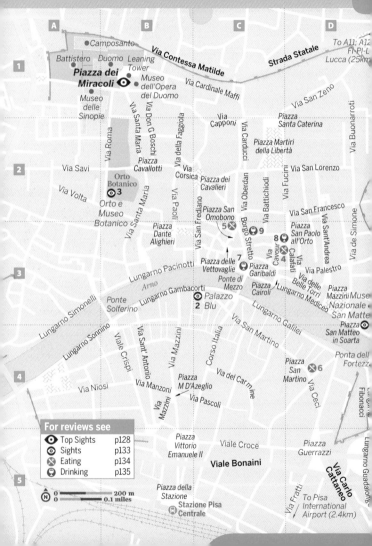

To A11; A12
FI-PI-L
Lucca (25km)

Camposanto
Via Contessa Matilde
Strada Statale

Battistero Duomo Leaning
Tower
**Piazza dei
Miracoli** ⊙
Via Cardinale Maffi
Museo
dell'Opera
del Duomo
Museo
delle
Sinopie

Via San Zeno
Via Buonarroti

Via
Capponi
Piazza
Santa Caterina

Via
Corsica
Piazza dei
Cavalieri
Via Carducci
Piazza Martiri
della Libertà

Via Savi
Piazza
Cavallotti
Orto
Botanico
⊙3
Orto e
Museo
Botanico
Via Santa Maria
Via Roma
Via Don G Boschi
Via della Faggiola
Via San Lorenzo
Via San Francesco
Via Sant'Andrea
Via de Simone

Via Volta
Piazza San
Omobono
5 ⊗
Via San Frediano
Via Paoli
Oberdan
Borgo Stretto
Via Battichiodi
Via Fucini
Piazza
San Paolo
all'Orto
8 ⊗
4
Via
Calatai

Piazza
Dante
Alighieri
Piazza delle
Vettovaglie
7
Piazza
Garibaldi
Via delle
Belle Torri
Via Cavour
Via Palestro
Piazza
Mazzini Museo
Nazionale
San Matte

Lungarno Pacinotti
Arno
Ponte di
Mezzo
Piazza
Cairoli
Lungarno Mediceo
Piazza
San Matteo
in Soarta

Ponte
Solferino
Lungarno Simonelli
Lungarno Gambacorti
Palazzo
2 Blu ⊙
Lungarno Galilei
Ponta dell
Fortezz

Lungarno Sonnino
Via Sant'Antonio
Via Mazzini
Corso Italia
Via San Martino
Piazza
San
Martino
⊗6
Via Ceci
Lu
Fibonacci

Via Niosi
Via Manzoni
Via
Mazzini
Piazza
M D'Azeglio
Via del Carmine
Via Pascoli

Piazza
Vittorio
Emanuele II
Viale Croce
Viale Bonaini
Piazza
Guerrazzi
Via Carlo
Cattaneo
Lungarno Guadalo

For reviews see	
⊙ Top Sights	p128
⊙ Sights	p133
⊗ Eating	p134
🍷 Drinking	p135

Ⓝ 0 ────── 200 m
  0 ────── 0.1 miles

Piazza della
Stazione
Stazione Pisa
Centrale

To Pisa
International
Airport (2.4km)
Via Fratti

Sights

Museo Nazionale di San Matteo MUSEUM

1 Map p132, D3

This inspiring repository of medieval masterpieces sits in a 13th-century Benedictine convent on the Arno's northern waterfront boulevard. The museum's collection of paintings from the Tuscan school (c 12th to 14th centuries) is notable, with works by Lippo Memmi, Taddeo Gaddi, Gentile da Fabriano and Ghirlandaio. Don't miss Masaccio's *St Paul*, Fra' Angelico's *Madonna of Humility* and Simone Martini's *Polyptych of Saint Catherine*. (📞050 54 18 65; Piazza San Matteo in Soarta 1; adult/reduced €5/2.50; 🕑8.30am-7.30pm Tue-Sat, to 1.30pm Sun)

Palazzo Blu GALLERY

2 Map p132, C3

Facing the river is this magnificently restored 14th-century building with a striking dusty-blue facade. Inside, its over-the-top 19th-century interior decoration is the perfect backdrop for the Foundation Pisa's art collection – predominantly Pisan works from the 14th to the 20th centuries on the 2nd floor, plus various temporary exhibitions (adult/reduced €6/4) on the ground floor. Admission also includes an **archaeological area** in the basement and the noble **residence** of this aristocratic palace, furnished as it would have been in the 19th

Orto e Museo Botanico

century, on the 1st floor. (www.palazzoblu. it; Lungarno Gambacorti 9; admission free; 🕑10am-7pm Tue-Fri, to 8pm Sat & Sun)

Orto e Museo Botanico GARDENS

3 Map p132, B2

For a Zen respite from the Piazza dei Miracoli crowd, explore this peaceful walled garden laced with centurion palm trees, flora typical to the Apuane Alps, a fragrant herb garden, vintage greenhouses and 35 orchid species. Showcasing the botanical collection of Pisa University, the garden dates to 1543 and was Europe's first university botanical garden, tended by the illustrious botanist Luca Ghini

(1490–1556). The museum, inside **Palazzo della Conchiglie**, explores the garden's history, with exquisite botanical drawings, catalogues, maquettes etc. (Botanical Garden & Museum; 050 221 13 10; Via Roma 56; adult/reduced/family €4/2/6; 8.30am-8pm Apr-Sep, 9am-5pm Mon-Sat, to 1am Sun Oct-Mar)

Eating

Osteria Bernardo

TUSCAN **€€**

4 Map p132, C3

This small bistro on a pretty square, well away from the Leaning Tower crowd, is the perfect fusion of easy dining and gourmet excellence. Its menu is small – just four or five dishes per course – and the cuisine is creative. Think pistachio-crusted lamb, beef in beer sauce or a tasty risotto with Stilton cheese, lettuce and crisp leek. Reservations recommended. (050 57 52 16; Piazza San Paolo all'Orto 1; meals €40; 8-11pm Tue-Sat, 12.30-2.30pm & 8-11pm Sun)

Pizzeria Il Montino

PIZZA **€**

5 Map p132, C3

There's nothing fancy about this down-to-earth pizzeria, an icon among Pisans, students and sophisticates alike. Take away or order at the bar then grab a table, inside or out, and munch on house specialities such as *cecina* (chickpea pizza), *castagnaccio* (chestnut cake) and *spuma* (sweet, nonalcoholic drink). Or go for a *focaccine* (small flat roll) filled with salami, pancetta or *porchetta* (suckling pig). (050 59 86 95; www.pizzeriailmontino.com; Vicolo del Monte 1; pizza €6-8.50, foccacine €2.50-5; 10.30am-3pm & 5-10pm Mon-Sat)

Ristorante Galileo

TUSCAN **€€**

6 Map p132, D4

For good, honest, unpretentious Tuscan cooking, nothing beats this classical old-timer. From the cork-covered wine list to the complimentary plate of warm homemade focaccia and huge platters of tempting *cantuccini* (almond-studded biscuits), Galileo makes you feel welcome. Fresh pasta is strictly hand- and homemade, and most veggies are plucked fresh that

Local Life

Keith

Trendy cafe **Keith** (050 50 31 35; www.facebook.com/keithcafe; Via Zandonai 4; 7am-11pm summer, to 9pm winter;) stares face to face with *Tuttomondo* (1989), the last wall mural American pop artist Keith Haring painted just months before his death on the facade of a Pisan church. Sip a coffee or cocktail on the terrace and lament the fading, weather-beaten colours of Haring's 30 signature prancing dancing men. Free wi-fi, occasional contemporary-art exhibitions, superb coffee and a student-friendly €5 *apericena* (*aperitivo* and dinner) buffet keep Keith buzzing.

morning from the restaurant's garden. (📞050 2 82 87; www.ristorantegalileo.com; Via San Martino 6-8; meals €25; ⏱12.30-2.30pm & 7.30-10.30pm Wed-Mon)

Drinking

Bazeel
BAR

7 🚇 Map p132, C3

A dedicated all-rounder, Bazeel is a hot spot from dawn to dark. Laze over breakfast, linger over a light buffet lunch or hang out with the A-list crowd over a generous *aperitivo* spread, live music and DJs. Its chapel-like interior is nothing short of fabulous, as is its pavement terrace out the front. Check its Twitter feed for what's on. (📞349 088 06 88; www.bazeel.it; Lungarno Pacinotti 1; ⏱7am-1am Sun-Thu, to 2am Fri & Sat)

Sottobosco
CAFE

8 🚇 Map p132, C3

This creative book-cafe is a breath of fresh air. Tuck into an end-of-day sugar doughnut and cappuccino or an early-evening *aperitivo* at a glass-topped table filled with artists' crayons perhaps, or a button collection. Salads, *panini,* salami or cheese *taglieri* (tasting boards) and oven-baked cheese are simple and homemade. Come dark, jazz bands play or DJs spin tunes. (📞050 314 20

Top Tip

The Best Ice in Town

Follow the crowd to world-class **Gelateria De' Coltelli** (Map p132, B3; 📞345 481 19 03; www.decoltelli.it; Lungarno Pacinotti 23; cones/tubs €2.30-4.50; ⏱11.30am-10.30pm Sun-Thu, to 11.30pm Fri & Sat), famed for its sensational artisanal, organic and 100% natural gelato. Flavours are as zesty and appealing as its bright-orange interior. The hard part is choosing: ginger, ricotta cheese with pine nuts and honey, candied chestnuts, almond with candied lemon peel, cashew with Maldon salt, kiwi, or ricotta with candied orange peel and chocolate chips.

84; www.facebook.com/sottobosco.libricafe; Piazza San Paolo all'Orto 3; ⏱noon-3pm & 6pm-midnight Tue-Fri, 6pm-1am Sat, to midnight Sun summer, reduced hours winter)

Caffè Pasticceria Salza
CAFE

9 🚇 Map p132, C3

This old-fashioned cake shop has been tempting Pisans into sugar-induced wickedness since 1898. It's an equally lovely spot for a cocktail – any time. Check its Facebook page for enticing foodie events and happenings. (📞050 58 01 44; Borgo Stretto 44; ⏱8am-8.30pm Tue-Sun)

Top Sights
Lucca

Getting There

🚃 **Train** From Florence (€7.50 to €9.60, 1¼ to 1¾ hours, hourly). In Lucca, follow the path across the moat.

🚗 **Car** A11 from Florence. Park in Parcheggio Carducci near Porta Sant'Anna.

Lovely Lucca endears itself to everyone who visits. Hidden behind imposing Renaissance walls, its cobbled streets, handsome piazzas and shady promenades make it a perfect destination to explore by foot. The city squirrels away a stunning portfolio of Romanesque churches and its laid-back, alfresco cafe life – perfect for relaxing over a coffee or glass of Lucchesi wine and a slow progression of rustic dishes prepared with fresh produce from the surrounding countryside – is second-to-none.

Entrance to Piazza dell'Anfiteatro

City Walls

Lucca's monumental *mura* (wall; 12m high, 4km long) was built around the old city in the 16th and 17th centuries. Its ramparts are crowned with a tree-lined footpath – a local favourite for a bike ride, picnic and sacrosanct *passeggiata* (early-evening stroll). **Biciclette Poli** and **Cicli Bizzarri** on Piazza Santa Maria hire bikes (per hour/day €3/15; 9am to 7pm summer).

Cattedrale di San Martino

This predominantly Romanesque **cathedral** (☎0583 49 05 30; www.museocattedralelucca.it; Piazza San Martino; adult/reduced €3/2, incl Museo della Cattedrale & Chiesa e Battistero dei SS Giovanni & Reparata €9/5; ☺9.30am-6pm Mon-Fri, to 6.45pm Sat, noon-6pm Sun summer, 9.30am-5pm Mon-Fri, to 6.45pm Sat, noon-6pm Sun winter) dates to the start of the 11th century. Inside, the **Volto Santo** is a simply fashioned Christ on a wooden crucifix that dates from the 13th century.

Torre Guinigi

The bird's-eye view from the top of this medieval, 45m-tall red-brick tower is magnificent – as are the seven oak trees planted in a U-shaped flower bed at the top. Count 230 steps up.

Palazzo Pfanner

Take a stroll around this beautiful, 17th-century **palace** (☎0583 95 21 55; www.palazzopfanner.it; Via degli Asili 33; palace or garden adult/reduced €4.50/4, both €6/5; ☺10am-6pm Apr-Nov) where parts of Jane Campion's *The Portrait of a Lady* (1996) were shot. Highlights include the frescoed, furnished *piano nobile* (main reception room) and the enchanting baroque-styled garden with ornamental pond, lemon house and 18th-century statues of Greek gods posing between potted lemon trees.

Tourist office

☎0583 58 31 50

www.turismo.lucca.it

Piazzale Verdi

☺9am-7pm Apr-Sep, to 5pm Mar-Oct

☑ Top Tips

▶ Stroll boutique-filled **Via Fillungo**; duck down a side street off its northeastern end to uncover oval-shaped **Piazza dell'Anfiteatro**, named after an amphitheatre located here in Roman times.

✗ Take a Break

▶ For picnic provisions, go to **Forno Amedeo Giusti** (☎0583 49 62 85; www.facebook.com/PanificioGiusti; Via Santa Lucia 20; pizzas & filled focaccias per kg €10-15; ☺7am-7.30pm Mon-Sat, 4-7.30pm Sun) for fresh-from-the-oven pizza and *focaccia* or **Da Felice** (☎0583 49 49 86; www.pizzeriadafelice.it; Via Buia 12; focaccia €1-3, pizza slices €1.30; ☺11am-8.30pm Mon, 10am-8.30pm Tue-Sat) for *cecina* (salted chickpea pizza) and *castagnacci* (chestnut cakes).

Explore

Siena

Unesco includes Siena's *centro storico* (historical centre) in its famed World Heritage list, citing it as the living embodiment of a medieval city. Easily explored in a day, the glories of its Gothic architecture and art provide a fascinating contrast to the Renaissance splendour that is so evident in Florence, making it a compelling side trip.

The Sights in a Day

🔅 Upon arrival, make a beeline for **Piazza del Campo** (pictured left; p145) and join locals sipping espressos at **Bar Il Palio** (p149) on Siena's most famous square. Spend the rest of the morning devouring peerless 14th-century secular art in the magnificent **Museo Civico** (p145). Hike up the **Torre del Mangia** (pictured left; p147) for a sensational Siena panorama.

🔅 Buy a prosciutto-fuelled picnic from **La Prosciutteria** (p148), tuck into lunch at staunchly local **Osteria Il Vinaio** (p148) or indulge in exquisite regional produce at upmarket **La Taverna di San Giuseppe** (p148). Afterwards, visit the cathedral, baptistry et al at the Opera della Metropolitana di Siena (p140). Nip into the **Museale Santa Maria della Scala** (p147) to admire the famous Pilgrim's Hall and complete the afternoon with a swoon-worthy gelato from **La Vecchia Latteria** (p148).

🌙 Before returning to Florence, mingle with Gothic masterpieces at art gallery **Pinacoteca Nazionale** (p145) or flop in the green **Orto de' Pecci** (p150) or **Orto Botanico** (p147). Celebrate your day with a glass of Tuscan wine at **Enoteca Italiana** (p149), inside the city's Medici Fortress.

 Top Sights

Opera della Metropolitana di Siena (p140)

❤️ **Best of Siena**

Art

Duomo (p141)

Museo Civico (p145)

Museo dell'Opera (p142)

Pinacoteca Nazionale (p145)

Eating

La Taverna di San Giuseppe (p148)

Views

Torre del Mangia (p147)

Panorama del Facciatone (p143)

Getting There

🚌 **Bus** Frequent express buses leave from Florence's SITA bus station (€7.80, 1¼ hours).

🚗 **Car** Florence–Siena speedy S2 or more scenic SR222. Park (€1.70 per hour) in car parks at San Francesco, Stadio Comunale, Fortezza Medicea and Santa Caterina.

Top Sights
Opera della Metropolitana di Siena

Siena's *duomo* is one of Italy's greatest Gothic churches, and the focal point of important ecclesiastical buildings that include a museum, baptistry and crypt. All are embellished with wonderful art – Giovanni and Nicola Pisano, Pinturicchio, Jacopo della Quercia, Ghiberti, Donatello and (most famous of Sienese painters) Duccio di Buoninsegna are some of the artists whose works glorified their city and their god.

Cattedrale di Santa Maria Assunta

◉ Map p144, B4

www.operaduomo.siena.it

Piazza Duomo

summer/winter €4/free, when floor displayed €7

🕑 10.30am-7pm Mon-Sat, 1.30-6pm Sun summer, to 5.30pm winter

Sculptures by Giovanni Pisano in the Museo dell'Opera (p142)

Duomo

Construction of the *duomo* started in 1215 and work continued well into the 14th century. The magnificent facade of white, green and red marble was designed by Giovanni Pisano; the statues of philosophers and prophets are copies; you'll find the originals in the Museo dell'Opera (p142). The interior is truly stunning, with walls and pillars continuing the black-and-white-stripe theme of the exterior.

Libreria Piccolomini

Through a door from the north aisle is this enchanting **library** (Piccolomini Library; ☎0577 28 63 00; http://operaduomo.siena.it; Piazza Duomo; summer/winter free/€2; ⏲10.30am-7pm Mon-Sat, 1.30-6pm Sun summer, to 5.30pm winter), built to house the books of Enea Silvio Piccolomini, better known as Pope Pius II. Its walls are decorated with richly detailed frescoes painted between 1503 and 1508 by Bernardino (di Betto) Pinturicchio and depicting events in the life of Piccolomini, including his ordination as pope.

Pisano's Pulpit

The *duomo's* exquisitely crafted marble-and-porphyry pulpit was created between 1265 and 1268 by Nicola Pisano, who had previously carved the famed pulpit in Pisa's *duomo*. Assisted by his son Giovanni and assistant Arnolfo di Cambio, Pisano depicted powerful scenes including the Last Judgement.

The Floor Panels

The inlaid-marble floor, decorated with 56 panels by about 40 artists and executed from the 14th to the 19th centuries, depicts historical and biblical subjects. Unfortunately, about half of the panels are obscured by protective covering, and are revealed only between late August and October each year (extra fee applies).

☑ Top Tips

▶ You'll save money (up to €9) by purchasing a combined OPA SI or Acropoli Pass, valid for three days, rather than individual tickets.

▶ The excellent two-hour, guided 'Classic Siena' walking tour offered by **Centro Guide Turistiche Siena e Provincia** (☎0577 4 32 73; www.guidesiena.it) includes a tour of the Duomo (Monday to Saturday) or Cripta (11am daily April to October).

✕ Take a Break

▶ From the *battistero*, head towards Piazza Independenza for a sophisticated lunch at **Enoteca I Terzi** (☎0577 4 43 29; www.enotecaiterzi.it; Via dei Termini 7; meals €35; ⏲11am-3pm & 6.30pm-1am Mon-Sat, shorter hours in winter).

▶ Stop by Il Magnifico (p150) to pick up some almond biscuits to fuel your museum wandering.

Understand
Pius II

Born Enea Silvio Piccolomini in the village of Corsignano (now Pienza) south of Siena, Pope Pius II (1405–64) was a tireless traveller, noted Humanist, talented diplomat, exhaustive autobiographer (13 volumes!) and medieval urban-planning trendsetter. Also a scholar, poet and writer of erotic and comic stories, Pius built a huge personal library that was relocated to the purpose-built Libreria Piccolomini (Piccolomini Library; p141) in Siena's *duomo* after his death by order of his nephew, Cardinal Francesco Todeschini Piccolomini, the future pope Pius III.

Battistero di San Giovanni

Behind the *duomo*, down a steep flight of steps, is the frescoed **baptistry** (Map p144; ☏0577 28 63 00; http://operaduomo.siena.it; Piazza San Giovanni; €4; ☉10.30am-7pm Mon-Sat, 1.30-6pm Sun summer, to 5.30pm winter). At its centre is a hexagonal marble font (c 1417) by Jacopo della Quercia, decorated with bronze panels depicting the life of St John the Baptist by artists including Lorenzo Ghiberti (*Baptism of Christ* and *St John in Prison;* 1427) and Donatello (*The Head of John the Baptist Being Presented to Herod;* 1427).

Cripta

This **space** (☏0577 28 63 00; http://operaduomo.siena.it; Piazza San Giovanni; incl audioguide €6; ☉10.30am-7pm Mon-Sat & 1.30-6pm Sun summer, to 5.30pm winter) below the cathedral's pulpit was rediscovered and restored in 1999 after having been filled to the roof with debris in the 1300s. The walls are completely covered with *pintura a secco* ('dry painting', better known as 'mural painting') dating back to the 1200s. There's some 180 sq metres worth, depicting biblical stories including the Passion of Jesus and the Crucifixion.

Museo dell'Opera

The collection in this **museum** (Map p144; ☏0577 28 63 00; www.operaduomo.siena.it; Piazza Duomo; €8; ☉10.30am-7pm Mon-Sat, 1.30-6pm Sun summer, to 5.30pm winter) showcases artworks that formerly adorned the *duomo*, including the 12 statues of prophets and philosophers (1285–87) by Giovanni Pisano that decorated its facade. Pisano designed these to be viewed from ground level, which is why they look so distorted as they crane uncomfortably forward. Also notable is the vibrant stained-glass window designed and painted by Duccio di Buoninsegna (1287–90).

Duccio's Maestà

Taking centre stage in the Museo dell'Opera del Duomo's collection is Duccio di Buoninsegna's striking *Maestà* (1308–11), which was painted on both sides as a screen for the *duomo's* high altar. The main painting portrays the Virgin surrounded by angels and saints; the rear panels (sadly

Frescoes on the ceiling of the Museo dell'Opera

incomplete) portray 26 scenes from the Passion of Christ.

Panorama del Facciatone

In 1339 the city's leaders decided to transform the cathedral into one of Italy's biggest churches, but the plague of 1348 scotched their plan to build an immense new nave with the present church as the transept. Known as the Duomo Nuovo (New Cathedral), all that remains of the project is this **panoramic terrace** (☎0577 28 63 00; http://operaduomo.siena.it; Piazza Duomo; ☉10.30am-7pm Mon-Sat, 1.30-6pm Sun summer, to 5.30pm winter), accessed through the museum.

Porta del Cielo

To enjoy spectacular bird's-eye views of the interior and exterior of Siena's cathedral, buy a ticket for the **Gate of Heaven** (Gate of Heaven; http://operaduomo. siena.it; Duomo; €15 Mar-Oct, €10 Nov-Feb; ☉10.30am-7pm Mon-Sat, 1.30-6pm Sun summer, 10.30am-5.30pm Mon-Sat, 1.30-5.30pm Sun winter) escorted tour up, into and around the building's roof and dome. Tour groups are capped at 18 participants and depart at fixed times throughout the day – purchase your ticket from the office in Santa Maria della Scala. Note that you'll need to arrive at the meeting point at least five minutes before your allocated tour time.

| A | B | C | D |

8 ❌ 🅑14
Piazza Gramsci
Via della Stufa Secca
Via dei Montanini
Via di Vallerozzi

For reviews see
👁	Top Sights	p140
👁	Sights	p145
❌	Eating	p148
🅑	Drinking	p149
🔒	Shopping	p150

Viale dello Stadio
Viale Frederico Tozzi

Stadio Comunale

🅿

Piazza Matteotti
Via Pianigiani
Piazza Salimbeni

Via del Paradiso
Costa dell'Incrociata

Piazza Provenzano Salvani

To Fortezza Medicea (500m)
Via della Sapienza
Via dei Banchi di Sopra
Via delle Terme
Via dei Termini

🅑13
🅑19
Piazza San Domenico
Via Camporegio
Costa di Sant'Antonio

Piazza Tolomei
Via Cecco Angolieri

👁6
Basilica di San Domenico
Via Santa Caterina
Via della Galluzza

Piazza Indipendenza
Banchi di Sotto

Vic delle Scotte
Via di Pantanet

🅑12
17🔒
Via di Fontebranda
Piazza del Campo
Via del Porrione
10 ❌

Battistero di San Giovanni
Via dei Pellegrini
🔒16
①
2👁
Museo Civico

Piazza San Giovanni
Museo dell'Opera
👁
Piazza del Mercato
15

Opera della Metropolitana di Siena 👁
Duomo
Via del Castoro
Piazza Jacopo della Quercia
Via di Salicotto

Piazza di Selva
4👁
Piazza Duomo
Via del Capitano
Via del Castoro

Museale Santa Maria della Scala
Via di Città
Via del Casato di Sotto
Via Giovanni Duprè
Via del Sol

Casato di Sopra
Via S Agata

Piazza di Postierla
11
9 ❌
Via San Pietro
Orto de' Pecci

18🔒
Piazza delle Due Porte
Via di Stalloreggi
Pinacoteca Nazionale
3👁
7👁

Via Paolo Mascagni
Via di Castelvecchio
5👁
Via S Agata

0 —— 200 m
0 —— 0.1 miles
Ⓝ

Sights

Piazza del Campo

SQUARE

1 Map p144, C3

Popularly known as 'Il Campo', this sloping piazza has been Siena's civic and social centre since being staked out by the ruling Consiglio dei Nove (Council of Nine) in the mid-12th century. Built on the site of a Roman marketplace, its paving is divided into nine sectors representing the number of members of the *consiglio* and these days acts as a carpet on which young locals meet and relax. The cafes around its perimeter are the most popular coffee and *aperitivi* (pre-dinner drinks) spots in town.

Museo Civico

MUSEUM

2 Map p144, C4

Entered via the Palazzo Pubblico's **Cortile del Podestà** (Courtyard of the Podestà), this wonderful museum showcases rooms richly frescoed by artists of the Sienese school. Commissioned by the city's governing body rather than by the Church, some of the frescoes depict secular subjects – highly unusual at the time. The highlights are two huge frescoes: Ambrogio Lorenzetti's *Allegories of Good and Bad Government* (c 1338–40) and Simone Martini's celebrated *Maestà* (*Virgin Mary in Majesty*; 1315). (Civic Museum; ☎0577 29 22 32; Palazzo Pubblico, Piazza del Campo 1; adult/reduced €9/8; ⏲10am-6.15pm summer, to 5.15pm winter)

Torre del Mangia (p147)

Pinacoteca Nazionale

GALLERY

3 Map p144, C5

An extraordinary collection of Gothic masterpieces from the Sienese school sits inside the once grand, but now sadly dishevelled, 14th-century **Palazzo Buonsignori**. The highlights are on the 2nd floor, where magnificent works by Guido da Siena, Duccio (di Buoninsegna), Simone Martini, Niccolò di Segna, Lippo Memmi, Ambrogio and Pietro Lorenzetti, Bartolo di Fredi, Taddeo di Bartolo and Sano di Pietro are housed. (☎0577 28 11 61; http://pinacotecanazionale.siena.it; Via San Pietro 29; adult/reduced €4/2; ⏲8.15am-7.15pm Tue-Sat, 9am-1pm Sun & Mon)

Understand

Inside the Museo Civico

After purchasing your ticket, head upstairs to the **Sala del Risorgimento**, where late-19th-century frescoes serialise key events in the Risorgimento (reunification period). Continue through to the **Sala di Balìa** (Rooms of Authority), where frescoes by father-and-son Spinello and Parri Aretino recount episodes in the life of Pope Alexander III (the Sienese Rolando Bandinelli), including his clashes with the Holy Roman Emperor Frederick Barbarossa. Straight ahead is the **Sala del Concistoro** (Hall of the Council of Clergymen), dominated by the allegorical ceiling frescoes (1529–35) by the mannerist painter Domenico (di Pace) Beccafumi.

Through a vestibule to the left is the **Anticappella** (Chapel Entrance Hall) with frescoes painted in 1415 by Taddeo di Bartolo. These include figures representing the virtues needed for the proper exercise of power (Justice, Magnanimity, Strength, Prudence, Religion), and depictions of some of the leading Republican lights of ancient Rome. The **Cappella** (Chapel) contains a fine wooden choir and a fresco of the *Holy Family and St Leonard* by Il Sodoma, while the star attraction in the **Vestibolo** (Vestibule) is a bronze wolf, the symbol of Siena.

The vestibule leads into the **Sala del Mappamondo** (Hall of the World Map), which houses Simone Martini's powerful and striking *Maestà*, painted when he was only 21 years old. On the other side of the room is Martini's oft-reproduced fresco (1328–30) of Guidoriccio da Fogliano, a captain of the Sienese army.

The next room, the **Sala dei Nove** (Hall of the Nine), is where the ruling Council of Nine once met. It's decorated with Ambrogio Lorenzetti's fascinating fresco cycle, the *Allegories of Good and Bad Government* (c 1338–40). The central allegory portrays scenes with personifications of Justice, Wisdom, Virtue and Peace, all unusually depicted as women, along with scenes of criminal punishment and rewards for righteousness. Set perpendicular from it are the frescoes *Allegory of Good Government and Allegory of Bad Government,* which feature intensely contrasting scenes clearly set around Siena. The good depicts a sunlit, idyllic, serene city, with joyous citizens and a countryside filled with crops; the bad city is filled with vices, crime and disease.

Museale Santa Maria della Scala

MUSEUM

4 Map p144, B4

Built as a hospice for pilgrims travelling the Via Francigena, this huge complex opposite the *duomo* dates from the 13th century. Its highlight is the upstairs **Pellegrinaio** (Pilgrim's Hall), featuring vivid 15th-century frescoes by Lorenzo di Pietro (aka Vecchietta), Priamo della Quercia and Domenico di Bartolo. All laud the good works of the hospital and its patrons; the most evocative is di Bartolo's *Il governo degli infermi* (*Caring for the Sick*; 1440–41), which depicts many activities that occurred here. (☑0577 53 45 11, 0577 53 45 71; www.santamariadellascala. com; Piazza Duomo 1; adult/reduced €9/7; ⊙10am-5pm Mon, Wed & Thu, to 8pm Fri, to 7pm Sat & Sun, extended hours in summer)

Orto Botanico

GARDENS

5 Map p144, C5

The tranquil terraces of this botanical garden, which is spread over 2.5 hectares of the verdant Sant'Agostino Valley, provide a welcome escape from the tourist crowds and gorgeous views across the valley. Owned by the University of Siena, which operates a scientific field here, it features hothouses filled with tropical and subtropical species, a genus terrace, fruit trees and gardens planted with aromatic, medicinal and food plants. In total, over 1000 species are represented. Native and endangered species are also represented. (Botanical Garden; ☑0577 23 28 77; www.simus.unisi.it; Via Pier Andrea Mattioli 4; adult/reduced €5/2.50; ⊙10am-7pm Jul-Sep, to 5pm Mar-Jun, to 4pm Oct-Feb)

Top Tip

Bird's-Eye City View

On Siena's central square, scale the graceful **Torre del Mangia** (☑0577 29 23 43; www.enjoysiena.it; Palazzo Pubblico, Piazza del Campo 1; €10; ⊙10am-6.15pm summer, to 3.15pm winter) for killer bird's-eye views of the city laid out at your feet. Completed in 1348, this 87m-high red-brick-and-travertine bell tower is called the Tower of Eater after Giovanni di Balduccio, nicknamed 'Mangiaguadagni' ('Eat the Earnings'), who was employed by the municipality to beat the hours on its bell from 1347 to 1360.

Basilica di San Domenico

CHURCH

6 Map p144, A2

St Catherine was welcomed into the Dominican fold within this huge and austere 13th-century basilica. Inside, the **Cappella di Santa Caterina** (halfway down the wall to the right of the altar) contains frescoes by Il Sodoma and Andrea Vanni depicting events in the saint's life. Also here are 15th-century reliquaries containing Catherine's head and one of her fingers, as well as a nasty-looking chain that she is said to have flagellated herself with. (www.basilicacateriniana.com; Piazza San Domenico; admission free; ⊙7am-6.30pm Mar-Oct, 9am-6pm Nov-Feb)

Eating

La Taverna di San Giuseppe

TUSCAN €€€

7 Map p144, C5

Any restaurant specialising in beef, truffles and porcini mushrooms attracts our immediate attention, but not all deliver on their promise. Fortunately, this one does. A favoured venue for locals celebrating important occasions, it offers excellent food, an impressive wine list with plenty of local, regional and international choices, a convivial traditional atmosphere and efficient service. Love it. (☑0577 4 22 86; www.tavernasangiuseppe.it; Via Dupré 132; meals €45; ☉noon-2.30pm & 7-10pm Mon-Sat)

Osteria Il Vinaio

TUSCAN €

8 Map p144, B1

Wine bars are thin on the ground here in Siena, so it's not surprising that Bobbe and Davide's neighbourhood *osteria* (casual tavern serving simple food and drink) is so popular. Join the multi-generational local regulars for a bowl of pasta or your choice from the

Top Tip
Lunch Tip

Buy a prosciutto-stuffed *panini* to go from La Prosciutteria (p148) and head to the Orto de' Pecci for a garden picnic.

Top Tip
Bar Chat

Via Camollia and **Via di Pantaneto** are Siena's major bar and coffee strips. Though atmospheric, the bars lining the Campo (p145) are expensive if you sit at a table – consider yourself warned.

generous antipasto display, washed down with a glass or two of eminently quaffable house wine. (☑0577 4 96 15; Via Camollia 167; antipasti €6-13, pasta €6-7; ☉10am-10pm Mon-Sat)

La Vecchia Latteria

GELATO

9 Map p144, C5

Sauntering through Siena's historical centre is always more fun with a gelato in hand. Just ask one of the many locals who are regular customers at this *gelateria artigianale* (maker of handmade gelato) near the Pinacoteca Nazionale. Using quality produce, owners Fabio and Francesco concoct and serve fruity fresh or decadently creamy iced treats – choose from gelato or frozen yoghurt. (☑0577 05 76 38; Via San Pietro 10; gelato €2-3.50; ☉noon-8pm)

La Prosciutteria

SANDWICHES €

10 Map p144, D3

The name says it all. Prosciutto is the focus here, served in *panini* or on a *taglieri* (tasting board) – cheese is an optional extra. Order to take away (the Orto de' Pecci (p150) is close by), or claim one of the tables on the street and enjoy a glass of wine (€2.50), too. (☑ 5414325; www.laprosciutteria.com; cnr Via Pantaneto & Vicolo Magalotti; panino €4-7, tasting board €5-15; ⏰ 11.30am-9.30pm; 🛜)

Osteria Boccon del Prete

MODERN ITALIAN €€

11 Map p144, C5

As popular with locals as it is with tourists, this casual place near the Pinacoteca Nazionale serves Tuscan dishes with a modern twist. The interior features a rich red colour scheme and modern art – very different to most of the city's eateries. (☑ 0577 28 03 88; Via San Pietro 17; meals €25; ⏰ 12.15-3pm & 7.15-10pm Mon-Sat)

Drinking

Bar Il Palio

CAFE

12 Map p144, C3

Arguably the best coffee on the Campo; drink it standing at the bar or suffer the financial consequences. Service on the terrace, which is a popular *aperitivo* spot, can be excruciatingly slow. (☑ 0577 28 20 55; Piazza del Campo 47; ⏰ 8am-10pm, later in summer)

Enoteca Italiana

WINE BAR

13 Map p144, A2

The former munitions cellar and dungeon of this **Medici fortress** (Piazza Caduti delle Forze Armate; admission free; ⏰ 24hr) has been artfully transformed

---

Understand
The Palio

Dating from the Middle Ages, this spectacular annual event includes a series of colourful pageants and a wild horse race on 2 July and 16 August in which 10 of Siena's 17 *contrade* (town districts) compete for the coveted *palio* (silk banner).

The race is staged in the Campo. From about 5pm, representatives from each *contrada* parade in historical costume, all bearing their individual banners. For scarcely one exhilarating minute, the 10 horses and their bareback riders tear three times around a temporarily constructed dirt racetrack with a speed and violence that makes spectators' hair stand on end.

The race is held at 7.45pm in July and 7pm in August. Join the crowds in the centre of the Campo at least four hours before the start if you want a place on the rails. Alternatively, cafes in the Campo sell expensive places on their terraces; these can be booked through the **tourist office** (Map p144, B4; ☑ 0577 28 05 51; www.enjoysiena.it; Piazza Duomo 1, Santa Maria della Scala; ⏰ 9am-6pm summer, to 5pm winter) up to one year in advance.

into a classy *enoteca* (wine bar) that carries more than 1500 Italian labels. You can take a bottle with you, ship a case home or just enjoy a glass in the attractive courtyard or vaulted interior. (☎0577 22 88 43; www.enoteca-italiana.it; Fortezza Medicea, Piazza Libertà 1; ☺noon-7.30pm Mon & Tue, to midnight Wed-Sat)

Mad in Italy
WINE BAR

14 Map p144, B1

About as hip as Siena gets, this laid-back 'biobar' is popular with the student set. Decor is thrift-shop quirky,

---

Q Local Life
Flee the Crowd

When the tourist crowd gets too much, retire to the tranquil terraces, tropical hothouses, fruit orchards and aromatic medicinal-plant gardens of Siena's Orto Botanico (p147). Spread over 2.5 hectares, the botanical gardens proffer gorgeous view across the valley.

Or explore **Orto de' Pecci** (☎0577 22 22 01; www.ortodepecci.it; Via Porta Giustizia; admission free; ☺8.30am-10pm summer, reduced hours winter; 🚼), an urban oasis with a small vineyard, an organic farm that supplies the on-site **restaurant** (pizza €5-8, meals €20; ☺noon-2.30pm & 7.30-10pm Tue-Sun) with fruit and vegetables, plenty of animals (geese, goats, ducks and donkeys) and a scattering of site-specific contemporary artworks.

---

the vibe is friendly and there's often live music on Fridays and Saturdays. Choose from a good range of wine and spirits and consider eating, too – many of the imaginatively presented dishes (€6 to €10) are vegetarian and organic. (☎0577 4 39 81; Via Camollia 136-138; ☺11am-4pm Mon-Thu, to midnight Fri & Sat)

UnTUBO
CLUB

15 Map p144, D4

Live jazz acts regularly take the stage at this intimate club near the Campo, which is popular with students and the city's boho set. Check the website for a full events program – blues, pop and rock acts pop in for occasional gigs too. Note that winter hours are often reduced. (☎0577 27 13 12; www.untubo.it; Via del Luparello 2; cover charge varies; ☺6.30pm-3am Tue-Sat)

Shopping

Il Magnifico
FOOD

16 🔒 Map p144, C3

Lorenzo Rossi is Siena's best baker, and his *panforte* (spiced fruit and nut cake), *ricciarelli* (sugar-dusted chewy almond biscuits) and *cavallucci* (chewy biscuits flavoured with aniseed and other spices) are a weekly purchase for most local households. Try them at his bakery and shop behind the *duomo*, and you'll understand why. (☎0577 28 11 06; www.ilmagnifico.siena.it; Via dei Pellegrini 27; ☺7.30am-7.30pm Mon-Sat)

Panforte cake

Il Pellicano

CERAMICS

17 🔒 Map p144, B3

Elisabetta Ricci has been making traditional hand-painted Sienese ceramics for over 30 years. She shapes, fires and paints her creations, often using Renaissance-era styles or typical *contrade* (district) designs. Elisabetta also conducts lessons in traditional ceramic techniques. (📞 0577 24 79 14; www.siena-ilpellicano.it; Via Diacceto 17a; ⏰ 10.30am-7pm summer, hours vary in winter)

Bottega d'Arte

ART

18 🔒 Map p144, B5

Inspired by the works of Sienese masters of the 14th and 15th centuries,

artists Chiara Perinetti Casoni, Paolo Perinetti Casoni and Michelangelo Attardo Perinetti Casoni create exquisite icons in tempera and 24-carat gold leaf. Expensive? Yes. Worth it? You bet. (www.arteinsiena.it; Via di Stalloreggi 47; ⏰ hours vary)

Wednesday Market

MARKET

19 🔒 Map p144, A2

Spreading around Fortezza Medicea and towards the Stadio Comunale, this is one of Tuscany's largest markets and is great for cheap clothing; some food is also sold. (admission free; ⏰ 7.30am-2pm)

Top Sights
Chianti

Getting There

🚌 Take the SR222
(Via Chiantigiana).

Split between the provinces of Florence (Chianti Fiorentino) and Siena (Chianti Senese), this photogenic wine region is criss-crossed by an impossibly picturesque network of provincial secondary roads, some unsealed. An easy drive from Florence, you'll see immaculately maintained vineyards and olive groves, honey-coloured stone farmhouses, dense forests, graceful Romanesque *pieve* (rural churches), handsome Renaissance villas and imposing stone castles built by Florentine and Sienese warlords during the Middle Ages.

Castello di Brolio

Badia e Passignano

Chianti doesn't get much more atmospheric than this 11th-century Benedictine Vallombrosan abbey run by the legendary Antinori wine-making dynasty. Head here to visit the historic church and abbey buildings, admire the views and taste Antinori wines in the *enoteca* (wine bar) or neighbouring Michelin-starred **Osteria di Passignano** (www.osteriadipassignano.com).

Antinori nel Chianti Classico

To reach this strikingly contemporary **cellar complex** (☎ 0552 35 97 00; www.antinorichianticlassico.it; Via Cassia per Siena 133, Località Bargino; tour & tasting €25-50, bookings essential; ⌚ 10am-5pm Mon-Fri, to 5.30pm Sat & Sun winter, 6.30pm Sat & Sun summer) motor uphill to the main building, built into the hillside. One-hour guided tours finish with a tasting of three Antinori wines in an all-glass room suspended above barrels in the cellar.

Castello di Brolio

Home to the aristocratic Ricasoli family, this 11th-century **wine estate** (☎ 0577 73 02 80; www.ricasoli.it; Località Madonna a Brolio; garden, chapel & crypt €5, guided tours €8; ⌚ 10am-5.30pm mid-Mar–Nov, guided tours 10.30am-12.30pm & 2.30-5pm Tue-Sun) is the oldest in Italy. It opens its formal garden, panoramic terrace and small museum to day-trippers, along with an *osteria* (casual tavern) and a *cantina*.

Castello di Ama

Centuries-old winemaking traditions meet cutting-edge contemporary art at this 12th-century agricultural estate. Think vineyards, winery, boutique hotel, restaurant and sculpture park. Book **tours** (☎ 0577 74 60 69; www.castellodiama.com; Località Ama; guided tours adult/child under 16yr €15/free; ⌚ by appointment) in advance.

Tourist office

☎ 390 55853606, 0558 54 52 71

www.helloflorence.net

Piazza Matteotti 10, Greve in Chianti

⌚ 10.30am-1.30pm late Mar–mid-Oct, to 6.30pm Easter-Aug

☑ Top Tips

▶ If meat is your sin, include the foodie hilltop town of Panzano in Chianti – home to Tuscany's celebrity butcher Dario Cecchini – in your itinerary.

▶ Advance bookings are essential to visit Antinori nel Chianti Classico, Castello di Ama and the vineyards and cellar at Badia a Passignano.

✖ Take a Break

▶ Head to the picturesque hilltop village of **Volpaia** near Radda in Chianti to visit the *cantina* (wine cellar) of the Castello di Volpaia wine estate and break for lunch over a snack at **Bar Ucci** (www.bar-ucci.it) or traditional Tuscan at **Ristorante La Bottega** (www.labottegadivolpaia.it).

Top Sights
San Gimignano

Getting There

🚌 **Bus** To/from Florence (€6.80, 1¼ to two hours) Change in Poggibonsi.

🚗 **Car** Siena–Florence *superstrada* SR2 and SP1. Park in Parcheggio Montemaggio (€2 per hour).

As you crest the hill coming from the east, the 14 towers of this walled hilltop town look like a medieval Manhattan. Originally an Etruscan village, San Gimignano grew and became prosperous in the Middle Ages due to its location on the Via Francigena pilgrimage route. Sadly, many of its inhabitants died in the 1348 plague. Today, not even the plague would deter the swarms of summer daytrippers lured by the town's intact medieval streets and enchanting rural setting.

Piazza della Cisterna

Collegiata

San Gimignano's Romanesque cathedral is known as the **Collegiata** (Duomo; Basilica di Santa Maria Assunta; ☎0577 94 01 52; www.duomosangimignano. it; Piazza del Duomo; adult/reduced €4/2; ⏱10am-7pm Mon-Sat, 12.30-7pm Sun summer, 10am-4.30pm Mon-Sat, 12.30-4.30pm Sun winter), a reference to the college of priests who originally managed it. Parts of the building date back to the second half of the 11th century, but its remarkably vivid frescoes, which resemble a vast medieval comic strip, date from the 14th century.

Palazzo Comunale

The 13th-century **Palazzo Comunale** (☎0577 99 03 12; www.sangimignanomusei.it; Piazza del Duomo 2; combined Civic Museums ticket adult/reduced €9/7; ⏱10am-7.30pm summer, 11am-5.30pm winter) has always been the centre of San Gimignano's local government; its magnificently frescoed Sala di Dante is where the great poet addressed the town's council in 1299 and its Camera del Podestà and Pinacoteca (Art Gallery) once housed government offices – now they are home to wonderful artworks. Be sure to climb the 218 steps of the *palazzo's* 54m **Torre Grossa** for a spectacular view over the town and surrounding countryside.

Galleria Continua

This commercial **art gallery** (☎0577 94 31 34; www.galleriacontinua.com; Via del Castello 11; admission free; ⏱10am-1pm & 2-7pm) – one of Europe's best – exhibits the work of big-name artists such as Ai Weiwei, Daniel Buren, Antony Gormley and Mona Hatoum. Spread over four venues (an old cinema, a medieval tower, a vaulted cellar and an apartment on Piazza della Cisterna), it's one of San Gimignano's most compelling attractions.

Tourist office

☎0577 94 00 08

www.sangimignano.com

Piazza del Duomo 1

⏱10am-1pm & 3-7pm summer, 10am-1pm & 2-6pm winter

☑ Top Tips

▶ Ask at the tourist office about money-saving combined museum tickets; it also organises guided tours and takes booking for wine-tasting master classes in town.

▶ Be sure to sample local white wine Vernaccia di San Gimignano.

✗ Take a Break

▶ Try excellent pasta dishes and house Vernaccia at **Ristorante La Mandragola** (www. locandalamandragola.it).

▶ Grab a *panino* (sandwich) with locally sourced ingredients at **Dal Bertelli** (via Capassi 30) and a gelato at **Gelateria Dondoli** (www.gelateria-dipiazza.com).

The Best of
Florence & Tuscany

Duomo (p24)
JAVEN/SHUTTERSTOCK ©

Best Walks
Heart of the City

The Walk

Every visitor to Florence spends time navigating the cobbled medieval lanes that run between Via de' Tornabuoni and Via del Proconsolo but few explore them thoroughly, instead focusing on the major monuments and spaces. This walk will introduce you to some less visited sights and laneways.

Start Piazza della Repubblica

Finish La Terrazza Lounge Bar

Length 2km; two hours

Take a Break

Fashionable Via de' Tornabuoni is the heart of Florence's original cafe society. **Caffè Giacosa** (p57) and **Procacci** (p46) are great choices.

Piazza della Repubblica (p39)

❶ Piazza della Repubblica

Start with a coffee at one of the historic cafes on this 19th-century **square** (p39). Its construction entailed the demolition of a Jewish ghetto and produce market, and the relocation of nearly 6000 residents.

❷ Chiesa e Museo di Orsanmichele

Follow Via Calimala and Via Orsanmichele to reach this unique **church** (p39), created in the 14th century when the arcades of a century-old grain market were walled in and two storeys added.

❸ Mercato Nuovo

Back on Via Calimala, walk south to the 16th-century **Mercato Nuovo** (New Market), a covered marketplace awash with stalls. Look for Il Porcellino (The Piglet), a bronze statue of a boar – rub its snout to ensure your return to Florence!

❹ Palazzo Davanzati

On Via Porta Rossa is this 14th-century warehouse **residence** (p38) with its studded doors and central loggia. A few doors down, next to the Slowly bar, peep through the sturdy iron gate and up to admire ancient brick vaults.

❺ Chiesa di Santa Trìnita

Continue to Via de' Tornabuoni, the city's most famous shopping strip. Cross Piazza Santa Trìnita and duck into this **church** (p55) to admire its frescoed chapels.

❻ Via del Parione

Wander down this narrow street filled with old mansions (now apartments) and artisans workshops. Pop into paper marbler Alberto Cozzi at No 35r and puppet maker **Letizia Fiorini** (p60) to watch local artisans at work.

❼ Chiesa di Santissimi Apostoli

Backtrack to Via de' Tornabuoni and turn right, past 13th-century **Palazzo Spini-Feroni**, home of Salvatore Ferragamo's flagship store, to Borgo Santissimi Apostoli. A short way ahead on Piazza del Limbo is the Roman-esque **Chiesa dei Santissimi Apostoli** in a sunken square once used as a cemetery for unbaptised babies.

❽ Hotel Continentale

After browsing in specialist boutique **La Bottega dell'Olio** (p47) at No 4r on the same square, walk east and turn right into Vicolo dell' Oro. The sleek rooftop terrace **La Terrazza Lounge Bar** (p43) inside Hotel Continentale is the perfect spot for a sundowner with a Ponte Vecchio view.

Best Walks
Renaissance Florence

⚡ The Walk

This greatest-hits tour crams a huge amount of culture into a very tight timeline – you'll need to proceed at a cracking pace to see everything in four hours. Alternatively – and preferably – divide it over two days to ensure that you do all of the sights justice.

Start Museo delle Cappelle Medicee

Finish Basilica di Santa Croce

Length 3.2km; minimum four hours

✕ Take a Break

Piazza della Signoria is a hugely atmospheric spot for a coffee or drink. Popular pit stops include **Caffè Rivoire** (p34) or the cafe inside the **Gucci Museo** (p35).

Piazza della Signoria (p39) and Palazzo Vecchio (p38)

JAVEN/SHUTTERSTOCK ©

❶ Museo delle Cappelle Medicee

Start in the territory of Renaissance powerbrokers and art patrons, the Medici, who commissioned a number of self-aggrandising monuments in San Lorenzo. The greatest is this **mausoleum** (p68), partly designed by Michelangelo and containing some of his finest sculptures.

❷ Palazzo Medici-Riccardi

Cross Piazza San Lorenzo to reach this Medici **palace** (p70), commissioned by Cosimo the Elder and designed by Michelozzo. Admire its facade then head inside to see Benozzo Gozzoli's vivid frescoes in the Cappella dei Magi. Lunch at **Trattoria Mario** (p71); arrive by noon to snag a table.

❸ Galleria dell'Accademia

Ogle the work of art most synonymous with the Renaissance – Michelangelo's statue of *David* in this **art gallery** (p64). A powerful evocation of the Humanist principles that underpinned this period, it easily lives up to its huge reputation.

❹ Museo degli Innocenti

Make your way to the Brunelleschi-designed loggia of this 15th-century foundling hospital and Europe's first orphanage – today a cutting-edge **museum** (p70) – which architectural historians credit as one of the great triumphs of Renaissance architecture.

❺ Duomo

Head to the **Duomo** (p24) and, assuming you have prebooked your timed slot in advance, climb to the top of its red-tiled dome, another Brunelleschi masterpiece. The 360-degree city panorama is breathtaking.

❻ Piazza della Signoria

Head south down Via del Proconsolo then west to wander through the city's most spectacular **piazza** (p39), admiring the open-air sculptures under the **Loggia dei Lanzi** and noting the location of the Uffizi – repository of the world's pre-eminent collection of Renaissance art – for future visits.

❼ Basilica di Santa Croce

Trail pedestrianised Borgo dei Greci to reach this huge Franciscan **basilica** (p84) where Renaissance luminaries including Michelangelo, Machiavelli, Galileo and Ghiberti are buried. Ogle Giotto frescoes in its Cappella Bardi and admire Brunelleschi's exquisite Cappella de' Pazzi.

Best
Shopping

In medieval and Renaissance Florence, gold-smiths, silversmiths and shoemakers were as highly regarded as sculptors and artists. Today, Florentines are equally enamoured of design and artisanship and go out of their way to source quality goods. Most are also happy to pay what's required (usually a considerable amount) to *fare la bella figura* (cut a fine figure).

Fashion

Florentines take great pride in their dress and appearance, which is not surprising given the Italian fashion industry was born here. Guccio Gucci and Salvatore Farragamo got the haute-couture ball rolling in the 1920s, and the first Italian prêt-à-porter show was staged here in 1951.

Via de' Tornabuoni and its surrounding streets – especially Via della Vigna Nuova, Via della Spada and Borgo SS Apostoli – are home to upmarket designers from Italy and abroad. Some up-and-coming designers are also here, although most are across the river in the Oltrarno and Santa Croce.

Arts & Crafts

Cheap imported handbags are common, especially in the city's main leather market, Mercato Nuovo. But for serious shoppers keen to delve into a city synonymous with craftsmanship, there are ample traditional boutiques and *botteghe* (workshops) to visit. Many are in the neighbourhood of Oltrarno, south of the Arno.

Traditional artisan wares produced by hand or on centuries-old machinery include jewellery, leather goods (shoes, gloves, bags), fabrics and stationery including marbled paper and bound journals.

Best Fashion

Benheart Leather shoes and jackets by a talented, street-smart Florentine. (p58)

Boutique Nadine Super-chic vintage fashion. (p47)

Byørk Trendy concept store in the Oltrarno. (p125)

A Piedi Nudi nel Parco High-end, avant-garde designer fashion. (p47)

Patrizia Pepe Modern, colourful designs for women and children by this Florentine fashion house. (pictured above; p47)

Street Doing Italian vintage. (p75)

Leather sandals on display

Best Accessories

Angela Caputi Colourful resin jewellery (p35)

Aprosio & Co Jewellery and accessories crafted from zillions of tiny beads. (p59)

Grevi Romantic millinery boutique. (p59)

Penko Renaissance-inspired jewels and gems by third-generation jeweller Paolo Penko. (p76)

Best Food & Drink

La Bottega della Frutta Food shop bursting with boutique produce. (p59)

Obsequium Serious wine shop, with tastings. (p125)

Mercato Centrale Central covered food market in San Lorenzo. (p71)

Dolceforte Serious chocolate. (p60)

Best Souvenirs

Officina Profumo-Farmaceutica di Santa Maria Novella Herbal remedies and beauty products in a pharmacy from 1612. (p59)

Il Papiro Florence's signature, hand-marbled paper. (p35)

Clet Hacked street signs: limited editions of the real thing. (p110)

Lorenzo Villoresi Fragrances of Tuscany by Florence's master perfumer. (p110)

Mio Concept Nifty homeware and fashion accessories, many by local designers, to take home. (p59)

Best Arts & Crafts

Lorenzo Perrone Snow-white book sculptures by an Italian artist in residence. (p115)

&Co Exquisite calligraphy and beautiful objects for the home by Betty Soldi. (p115)

Scriptorium Hand-crafted leather books, boxes and wax seals in a *palazzo* boutique. (p75)

Fabriano Boutique Paper galore. (p35)

Letizia Fiorini Watch handmade puppets being made and buy the finished product. (p60)

Pineider Traditional Florentine stationery. (p60)

Best
Architecture

A trio of architectural styles are showcased in Florence: Romanesque, Tuscan Gothic and Renaissance. The latter originated here – before taking the rest of Italy and Europe by storm – and is the city's emblematic style.

JAVEN/SHUTTERSTOCK ©

Romanesque

A blow-in from Northern Europe, Romanesque architecture received a unique local twist in Tuscany, where church facades were given alternating stripes of green and white marble. Generally, Romanesque buildings displayed an emphasis on width and the horizontal lines of a building rather than height, and featured church groups with *campaniles* (bell towers) and baptistries that were separate to the church.

Gothic

Tuscans didn't embrace the Gothic as enthusiastically as their northern neighbours; the flying buttresses, grotesque gargoyles and over-the-top decoration were too far from the classical ideal that was bred in the Tuscan bone. There were, of course, exceptions; most notably Siena's *duomo* (cathedral).

Renaissance

When the dome of Florence's Duomo was completed in 1436, Leon Battista Alberti called it the first great achievement of the 'new' architecture, one that equalled or even surpassed the great buildings of antiquity. The elegance of line, innovation in building method and references to antiquity that characterised Brunelleschi's work were emulated by other Florentine architects, leading to this pared-down, classically inspired style dominating local architecture throughout the 15th and 16th centuries.

☑ **Top Tip**

▶ Guided walking tours of the city are a great way to learn about and appreciate its architecture. Recommended operators include **ArtViva** (☏ 055 264 50 33; www.italy.artviva.com; Via de' Sassetti 1; per person from €29) and Florence Town (p38).

Best Romanesque

Basilica di San Miniato al Monte 11th-century church with fine crypt. (p106)

Basilica di Santa Maria Novella Transitional from Romanesque to Gothic. (p50)

Piazza dei Miracoli (p128), Pisa

Battistero di San Giovanni Octagonal structure with striking green-and-white marble exterior. (p26)

Piazza dei Miracoli, Pisa Peerless example of a Romanesque cathedral group. (p128)

Cattedrale di San Martino, Lucca Unusual Romanesque facade and rebuilt Gothic interior. (p137)

Best Tuscan Gothic

Duomo, Siena Polychrome marble facade and black-and-white striped interior. (p140)

Duomo Exquisite facade and elegant *campanile* (bell tower). (pictured above left). (p24)

Museo Civico, Siena Inside the Palazzo Pubblico whose concave facade complements the convex curve of Piazza del Campo. (p145)

Best Renaissance

Duomo Brunelleschi's dome is considered the finest and most influential achievement of Renaissance architecture. (p24)

Museo degli Innocenti Classically elegant loggia. (p70)

Cappella de' Pazzi, Basilica di Santa Croce Sublimely beautiful exercise in architectural harmony. (p84)

Biblioteca Medicea Laurenziana Michelangelo's staircase pre-empts baroque curves. (p68)

Basilica di San Lorenzo Harmonious design with a particularly beautiful sacristy. (p68)

Museo delle Cappelle Medicee Sumptuous Michelangelo design where no cost was spared. (p68)

Palazzo Pitti Muscular design that shouts power and prestige. (p100)

Palazzo Medici-Riccardi The prototype of Renaissance civic architecture. (p70)

Palazzo Strozzi The last and most magnificent of the palaces built in the Renaissance. (p40)

Chiesa e Museo di Orsanmichele Unusual, largely unsung church once decorated with statues by some of the greatest Renaissance artists. (p39)

Best
Views

Best Views from Monuments

Campanile & Dome, Duomo 360-degree city views. (p24)

Galleria degli Uffizi Snapshots of riverside Florence. (p30)

Palazzo Vecchio Bird's-eye view atop crenellated Torre d'Arnolfo. (p38)

Leaning Tower, Pisa Admire Piazza dei Miracoli and the Apuane Alps beyond. (p129)

Torre del Mangia, Siena Vertiginous viewpoint of Campo action. (p147)

Panorama del Facciatone, Siena Quintessential, terracotta-coloured rooftop views. (p143)

Basilica di San Miniato al Monte Admire Florence laid out at your feet. (p106)

Museo degli Innocenti Lounge between chimney pots and sculptures in the museum's rooftop cafe with view extraordinaire. (p70)

Torre San Niccolò Blockbuster river views atop a 14th-century tower. (p106)

Best Views from Public Spaces

Piazzale Michelangelo See Florence unfurled from the city's most spectacular vantage point, preferably at sunset. (pictured above; p106)

Ponte Vecchio The most romantic sunset view in Florence. (p122)

Best Dining with a View

La Leggenda dei Frati Michelin-starred garden dining with impossibly romantic city panorama. (p107)

Santarosa Bistrot Pretty garden views in a hipster bistro-bar near the river. (p122)

Irene Front-row seats on Piazza della Repubblica. (p40)

La Reggia degli Etruschi, Fiesole Stupendous views over Florence. (p81)

Villa Aurora, Fiesole Fabulous Florentine panorama from a pagoda-covered lunch terrace. (p81)

KIATTISAK ANOOCHITAROM/SHUTTERSTOCK ©

San Niccolò 39 Summertime dining in a hidden garden in village-like San Niccolò. (p108)

Best View-Fuelled Drinks

La Terrazza Lounge Bar Chic setting in which to watch the sun set over the Arno. (p43)

La Terrazza Bird's-eye city views on the rooftop cafe of Florence's main department store. (p35)

Caffè Rivoire Box-seat view of Piazza della Signoria. (p34)

La Loggia Sweeping city views up high on Piazzale Michelangelo. (p109)

Best
Nightlife

BARONE FIRENZE/SHUTTERSTOCK ©

Hanging out on warm summer nights on cafe and bar terraces aside, Florence enjoys a varied nightlife scene thanks in part to its substantial foreign-student population. The city has highly regarded theatres and – from around midnight once *aperitivi* (pre-dinner drinks) and dinner are done – a fairly low-key but fun dance scene.

Best Dance Clubs

Flò Summer-only venue with themed lounge areas and a dance floor. (p109)

Bamboo Lounge and dance club in nightlife-hot Santa Croce. (p89)

Full Up Eternally popular club with the 20-something crowd, going strong since the 1950s. (p95)

Space Club Dancing, drinking and video-karaoke among a mixed, student-international crowd. (p58)

YAB Over 30s head here on Thursdays, students on other nights. (p46)

Best Live Performance Venues

Il Teatro del Sale Dinner followed by a performance of drama, music or comedy. (p89)

Le Murate Caffè Letterario Film screenings, book readings, live music and art exhibitions. (p94)

Volume Music, art and DJs in an old hat-making workshop. (p124)

Best Live Music

Dolce Vita Live bands cap off the packed after-dark agenda at this busy Oltrarno lounge bar. (p125)

Lion's Fountain Irish pub with live music. (p95)

Quelo Live bands in a 1950s vintage interior. (p95)

La Cité Vibrant alternative live-music space. (p124)

Chillax Lounge Bar Lounge-bar cocktails and live gigs covering all sounds. (p74)

Best Classical Music

Teatro della Pergola Classical concerts in a beautiful old city theatre. (p74)

Opera di Firenze The city's opera house, host to Florence's annual springtime Maggio Musicale Fiorentino festival. (pictured above; p58)

Best
Eating

Quality ingredients and simple execution are the hallmarks of Florentine cuisine, climaxing with the *bistecca alla fiorentina*, a huge slab of prime T-bone steak rubbed with tangy Tuscan olive oil, seared on the char grill, garnished with salt and pepper and served beautifully *al sangue* (bloody). Be it dining in a traditional trattoria or contemporary, designer-chic space, quality is guaranteed.

Cafes

Florentines don't pause long for *colazione* (breakfast). Most make a quick dash into a bar or cafe for an espresso and *cornetto* (croissant) standing at the bar. At *pranzo* (lunch), busy professionals will sometimes grab a quick snack at a cafe – usually a *panino* (sandwich) or *tramezzini* (the local version of a club sandwich) accompanied by a glass of wine or a coffee.

Trattorie, Osterie & Ristoranti

Champions of traditional Tuscan cuisine, these low-fuss eateries are greatly beloved in Florence. Popular for both *pranzo* and *cena* (dinner), they are often family run and excellent value for money. There's a fine line between an upmarket version of an *osteria* (casual tavern) or trattoria and *ristorante*; service is more formal in *ristoranti* and cuisine is generally more refined.

Enoteche

Enoteche (wine bars) are trending in today's Florence, popular for their focus on quality wine and light, seasonally driven dishes often described as 'Modern Tuscan'. Popular destinations for *aperitivi* (pre-dinner drinks), they are equally alluring for a casual *pranzo* or *cena*.

Best Traditional Tuscan

Trattoria Mario Sensational Tuscan dining by San Lorenzo market. (p71)

Trattoria Cibrèo Top-notch Tuscan cuisine à la Fabio Picchi in Sant'Ambrogio. (p92)

Trattoria Sergio Gozzi All the classics in an interior unchanged since 1915. (p72)

Osteria Il Buongustai Tasty Tuscan home cooking at a snip of other restaurant prices. (p41)

Trattoria Le Massacce Old-world home cooking every Tuscan Nonna would approve of. (p41)

Grom (p42)

La Taverna di San Giuseppe, Siena Quintessential Tuscan dining experience. (p148)

Best Modern Tuscan

Essenziale Inventive cuisine by one of Florence's most talented chefs. (p119)

Irene Creative bistro fare on Piazza della Repubblica. (p40)

Il Santo Bevitore Longstanding, modern Tuscan favourite on the Oltrarno. (p119)

iO Osteria Personale Creative *osteria* to die for. (p121)

La Leggenda dei Frati Michelin-starred gastronomy near Boboli Gardens. (p107)

Best Gelato

Gelateria Pasticceria Badiani Handmade gelato and sweet pastries, famed Italy-wide. (p44)

Grom Top-notch gelato near the Duomo. (p42)

Vivoli Vintage fave for coffee, cakes and gelato. (p94)

My Sugar Sensational artisan *gelateria* near Piazza San Marco. (p72)

Gelateria La Carraia Florentine favourite the other side of the river. (p122)

Best Panini

Semel Creative sandwiches to go in Sant'Ambrogio. (p92)

'Ino Gourmet *panini* near the Uffizi. (p42)

Mariano Favourite for its simplicity, in a 13th-century cellar since the 1970s. (p56)

Best Quick Bites

All'Antico Vinaio Mad-busy deli serving iconic cured-meat tasting platters. (p91)

La Toraia Riverside food truck cooking up artisan burgers. (p95)

Trippaio Sergio Pollini Tripe to go in foodie Sant'Ambrogio. (p93)

Raw Freshly made, raw snacks and dishes – all sensational – to eat in or go. (p120)

S.Forno Hipster bakery selling delicious breads, pastries and savoury snacks. (p121)

Best
Drinking

Florence's drinking scene covers all bases. Be it historical cafes, contemporary cafes with barista-curated specialist coffee, traditional *enoteche* (wine bars, which invariably make great eating addresses too), trendy bars with lavish *aperitivo* buffets, secret speakeasys and edgy cocktail or craft-beer bars, drinking is fun and varied.

OLIMAN/SHUTTERSTOCK ©

Cafes

Florence has cafes of every type – historic, hip, bohemian, cosy and plenty with no frills. Most are bar-cafe hybrids, serving beer, wine and spirits as well as coffee, along with pastries in the morning and *panini* (sandwich) at lunch. Those located on piazzas often have terraces that are perfect places for whiling away an hour or so.

Bars

You can drink at a bar almost any time of the day, but most are at their best from 5pm (aka *aperitivo* time), when many places serve complimentary snacks with drinks. *Apericena*, a brilliant cent-saving trick and trend among students and 20-somethings in Florence, translates as an *aperitivo* (pre-dinner drinks accompanied by cocktail snacks), buffet so copious it doubles as *cena* (dinner).

Enoteche (wine bars) take pride in their selection of wines and tend to concentrate on Tuscan labels. Most offer tempting *antipasto* platters of cheese, cured meats and crostini (toasts with various toppings) to eat; many serve light meals, too.

☑ Top Tips

▶ Join locals drinking their coffee standing at the cafe's *banco* (bar counter) – it is three to four times cheaper than a coffee ordered sitting at a table.

▶ There is one cardinal rule: milky coffee such as cappuccino, *caffe latte* or *latte macchiato* is only ever drunk in the early morning – never, ever, after a meal when the coffee to drink is strictly espresso.

Cafes on a piazza near Basilica di San Lorenzo (p68)

Best Cafes

Ditta Artigianale Hipster coffee roastery and gin bar. (p96)

Caffè Giacosa Chic, fashionista cafe with 1815 pedigree by Florence's smartest shopping strip. (p57)

Caffè Rivoire Legendary hot chocolate on Piazza della Signoria. (p34)

Le Murate Caffè Letterario Artsy cafe-bar in the city's former jail. (p94)

Gilli Historic cafe at home on Florence's old Roman forum; serious cakes. (p44)

Todo Modo Hip bookshop with cafe and pocket theatre. (p57)

Best Wine Bars

Enoteca Pitti Gola e Cantina Serious wine bar with tastings and food opposite Palazzo Pitti. (p123)

Le Volpi e l'Uva First-class food pairings with wines by boutique producers. (p109)

Il Santino Intimate, *aperitivo*-perfect wine bar just across the river. (p123)

Coquinarius Spacious and tasty *enoteca*, food to boot, near the Duomo. (p44)

Best Cocktail Bars

Mad Souls & Spirits Expertly mixed cocktails in San Frediano. (p123)

Rasputin Late-night cocktails in the secret speakeasy everyone knows about. (p123)

Lo Sverso Stunning cocktails, craft beer and homemade ginger ale in San Lorenzo. (p73)

Mayday Tuscan cocktails courtesy of the talented Marco. (p44)

Kawaii Creative, sake-based fusion cocktails and Japanese tapas. (p124)

Best Summer Terraces

Santarosa Bistrot Hipster garden bistro-bar beneath trees in Santarosa gardens. (p122)

Flò Summertime terrace bar with dancing, drinks and city views to die for. (p109)

La Terrazza Coffee atop the city's central department store. (p35)

La Terrazza Lounge Bar Rooftop chic in 1950s-styled design hotel by the river. (p43)

Best
Activities

Urban and art rich to the core, Florence is hardly a hardcore activity centre: cooking, rowing along the Arno or indulging in a morning jog along its grassy riverbanks, up narrow stone-walled lanes to San Miniato al Monte or in Parco delle Cascine is about as active as most Florentines get.

KANUMAN/SHUTTERSTOCK ©

Best Climbs

Campanile, Duomo 414 steps up Giotto's 85m belltower. (p26)

Cupola, Duomo 463 steps winding up the inside edge of Brunelleschi's extraordinary 114m dome. (p25)

Torre d'Arnolfo 418 steps up the Palazzo Vecchio's 94m tower. (p38)

Panorama del Facciatone, Siena 131 steps to the top of the never-finshed New Cathedral. (p143)

Leaning Tower, Pisa 300-odd steps up the world-famous but decidedly wonky 56m tower. (p129)

Torre del Mangia, Siena 87m high, with 500-odd steps. (p147)

Palazzo Comunale, San Gimignano 218 steps and 54m high up the Torre Grossa. (p155)

Best Guided Tours

ArtViva Urban walks and runs, some themed. (p164)

Florence Town Excellent one-stop shop for a range of city-based tours and activities. (p38)

Palazzo Vecchio Take the 'Secret Passages' or 'Experiencing the Palace First-Hand' tours. (p38)

Giardino Torrigiani Let an Italian aristocrat show you his garden. (p120)

Porta del Cielo, Duomo, Siena Escorted tours up, into and around the *duomo*'s roof and dome, with spectacular bird's-eye views. (p143)

Corridoio Vasariano Follow in the steps of the Medici from the Uffizi to Palazzo Pitti. (p38)

Best Passeggiatas

City Walls, Lucca Along the path atop this Renaissance-era wall. (p137)

Piazza del Campo, Siena Join the throng milling around in Siena's central sloping square. (p145)

Orto e Museo Botanico, Pisa Escape the tourist crowd with a leafy *passeggiata* in Pisa's peaceful botanical garden. (p133)

Via de' Tornabuoni Florence's most glamorous shopping strip. (p40)

Best
Romance

Few cities are as romantic as Florence. Come here to picnic in historic gardens, watch the sun set over the Arno or wander hand-in-hand through ancient cobbled streets. On the practical side, intimate restaurants with dinner tables for two are easy to find, as are luxury and designer hotels (many of these offer high levels of service and some have romantic accoutrements including panoramic terraces and tower suites).

CHRISTIAN MUELLER/SHUTTERSTOCK ©

Best Places to Stay

Ad Astra Contemporary-design guesthouse with romantic views over a historic walled garden. (p179)

Palazzo Vecchietti Hopelessly romantic rooms, some with private terraces. (p179)

Palazzo Magnani Feroni Opulent *palazzo*. (p179)

Hotel Orto de' Medici Enchanting midranger with intimate garden. (p179)

Best Restaurants

Enoteca Pinchiorri The ultimate seduction: triple Michelin-starred dining. (p93)

La Leggenda dei Frati Garden dining with sweeping Florence panorama. (p107)

Il Santo Bevitore Candlelit tables and Modern Tuscan cuisine. (p119)

Obicà Sofa seating in an elegant, star-topped courtyard. (p43)

Best Picnics

Santarosa Bistrot Grab a picnic to share in this riverside garden with your loved one. (p122)

La Toraia Lounge riverside over artisan burgers from this savvy food truck. (p95)

Best Intimate Strolls

Palazzo Pfanner, Lucca Mooch between lemon trees and Greek god statues in the intimate garden of a 17th-century palace. (p137)

Villa e Giardino Bardini Historic villa and gardens with ample secret nooks and crannies. (pictured above; p106)

City Walls, Lucca Experience the sacrosanct *passeggiata* atop 16th-century city walls. (p137)

Best Sunset Drinks

La Terrazza Lounge Bar Watch the sun set over the Arno over rooftop cocktails. (p43)

Ponte Santa Trìnita Snug up on a bridge; BYO. (p57)

La Loggia Sit beneath elegant arches and watch the sun set over the city. (p109)

Best
For Art

Florence has always embraced art and culture. Few artistic works remain from its days as a Roman colony, but plenty date from the Middle Ages, when the city first hit its artistic stride. Funded by medieval bankers, merchants and guilds, artists adorned the city's churches, *palazzi* (mansions) and public buildings with frescoes, sculptures and paintings of a quality never before encountered. This continued through the period now known as the Renaissance, bequeathing Florentines a truly extraordinary artistic heritage.

PETER VRABEL/SHUTTERSTOCK ©

Medieval Art

The Middle Ages get a bad rap in the history books. This period may have been blighted by famines, plagues and wars, but it also saw the rise of civic culture in the Italian city-states, a phenomenon that led to an extraordinary flowering of painting and sculpture. When the Gothic style was imported from Northern Europe, local artists reworked it into a uniquely Tuscan form, creating works that were both sophisticated and elegant and that highlighted attention to detail, a luminous palette and increasingly refined techniques.

Renaissance Art

During the 15th century, painting overtook its fellow disciplines of sculpture and architecture and became the pre-eminent art form for the first time in the history of Western art. Painters experimented with perspective and proportion and took a new interest in realistic portraiture. Supported by wealthy patrons such as the Medici, Florentine painters including Giotto di Bondone, Sandro Botticelli, Tommaso di Simone (Masaccio), Piero della Francesca, Fra' Angelico and Domenico Ghirlandaio were among many artistic innovators.

Best Frescoes

Basilica di Santa Maria Novella Panels by Ghirlandaio and Masaccio's *Trinity*. (p50)

Cappella Brancacci Masaccio's *The Expulsion of Adam and Eve from Paradise* and *The Tribute Money*. (p118)

Palazzo Medici-Riccardi Benozzo Gozzoli's *Journey of the Magi* in the Cappella dei Magi. (p70)

Museo di San Marco Fra' Angelico's galore, including his *Annunciation*. (p69)

Museo Civico, Siena Simone Martini's *Maestà* and Ambrogio Lorenzetti's *Allegories of Good and Bad Government*. (p145)

Detail of a fresco in Palazzo Medici-Riccardi (p70)

Collegiata, San Gimignano Taddeo di Bartolo's *The Last Judgment* and Domenico Ghirlandaio's *Santa Fina* panels. (p155)

Duomo, Siena Bernardino Pinturicchio's *Life of Pius II* in the Libreria Piccolomini. (p140)

Museo dell'Opera, Siena Duccio di Buoninsegna's *Maestà*. (p142)

Basilica di Santa Croce The Giotto panels in Cappella Bardi and Cappella Peruzzi. (p84)

Cenacolo di Sant'Apollonia Andrea del Castagno's *Last Supper*. (p72)

Best Paintings

Uffizi Gallery Paintings by every major Italian Renaissance artist. (p30)

Pinacoteca Nazionale, Siena Gothic masterpieces from the Sienese school. (p145)

Museo Nazionale di San Matteo, Pisa Paintings from the medieval Tuscan school. (p133)

Basilica di San Lorenzo Fra' Filippo Lippi's *Annunciation*. (p68)

Palazzo Pitti Stellar collection of 16th- to 18th-century works in Galleria Palatina. (p100)

Best Sculptures

Museo del Bargello Donatello's *Davids* and early Michelangelos. (p86)

Galleria dell'Accademia Michelangelo's *David* (pictured above left) and his *Prigioni* ('Prisoners' or 'Slaves'). (p64)

Museo delle Cappelle Medicee A trio of haunting Michelangelo sculptures. (p68)

Grande Museo del Duomo Ghiberti's *Door of Paradise* panels and Michelangelo's *La Pietà*. (p27)

Duomo & Battistero, Pisa Giovanni and Nicola Pisano's twinset of pulpits. (p129)

Palazzo Vecchio Michelangelo's *Genius of Victory* in the Salone dei Cinquecento. (p38)

Basilica di Santo Spirito Wooden crucifix attributed to Michelangelo. (p118)

Best
For Families

Children are welcomed anywhere, anytime in Florence. Families frequently go out with young children in the evenings, and pasta-rich dining is generally relaxed, straightforward and easy. Some museums run engaging themed tours and workshops, and there are several city parks and riverside paths for kids to run wild post-museum visit.

ALEXANDER SHCHUKIN/SHUTTERSTOCK ©

Best for Toddlers

Giardino di Boboli Statues, open spaces, hidden paths and a really weird 'face' sculpture. (p103)

Piazza della Repubblica Ride a vintage carousel. (p39)

Letizia Fiorini Watch traditional puppets being made. (p60)

Parco delle Cascine Open-air swimming pool and toddler-friendly playgrounds. (p55)

Best for Bigger Kids

Palazzo Strozzi Art workshops, tours and other artsy activities for families. (p40)

Palazzo Vecchio Climb the Torre d'Arnolfo and tour the palace's secret passages. (p38)

Duomo Climb up Giotto's bell tower or into Brunelleschi's dome. (p24)

Museo Galileo History of science museum; interactive displays. (p40)

Leaning Tower, Pisa Climb it. Push it. Prop it up with your foot. Selfie heaven. (pictured above; p129)

Caffè Rivoire Serious hot chocolate. (p34)

Best for Teenagers

Street Levels Gallery Gen up on the local street art scene. (p55)

FiesoleBike Cycle by sunset ride from Fiesole to Florence. (p81)

Aquaflor Learn about the exotic world of fragrance with a master perfumer. (p96)

 Top Tips

▶ Children with EU passports under 18 receive free entry to many museums.

▶ Many streets are too crowded and cobbled, pavements too narrow, to push a stroller along – bring a backpack carrier instead.

Clet Watch Florence's master street-sign hacker at work in his Oltrarno studio. (p110)

Il Trippaio del Porcellino Experience something new: *lampredotto* (cow's fourth stomach, chopped and simmered) from a traditional tripe truck. (p42)

Survival Guide

Survival Guide

Before You Go

When to Go

Florence

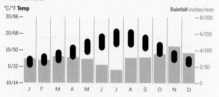

➡ **Spring** (April and May) The start of Florence's tourist season – the weather is pleasantly warm, cafe life spills outside, and many festivals are scheduled.

➡ **Summer** (June to August) Peak tourist season – the city gets hot and crowded in July; expect to queue for some museums. Many restaurants close in August.

➡ **Autumn and Winter** (September to March) A mellow time of year to visit, with with extraordinary light. Days are cold but often blue-skied. Accommodation bargains abound.

Book Your Stay

➡ Accommodation options include hostels, family-run *pensioni* (guesthouses), B&Bs, boutique hotels and luxury villa or *palazzo* (palace) hotels. It is always wise to book well ahead.

➡ Hotels are nonsmoking by national law and many offer accommodation for mobility-impaired guests.

➡ Cities and towns charge a *tassa di soggiorno* (hotel occupancy tax) on top of advertised hotel rates. It is always charged in addition to your hotel bill and must generally be paid in cash. The exact amount, which varies from city to city, depends on how many spangly stars your hotel is endowed with and the time of year. Expect to pay €1.50 per person per night in a one-star hotel or hostel, €2.50 in a B&B, €1.50 to €3.50 in an *agriturismo* (farm stay), €3.50 in a three-star hotel and up to €5 in a four- or five-star hotel.

Useful Websites

➜ **Lonely Planet** (lonelyplanet.com/ italy/florence/hotels) Recommendations and bookings.

➜ **Cross-Pollinate** (www.cross-pollinate. com) Personally vetted guesthouses, B&Bs and self-catering apartments.

➜ **Apartments Florence** (www.apartments florence.it) Just that.

➜ **Lungarno Collection** (www.lungarnocollection. com) Boutique collection of luxurious hotels owned by the Ferragamo fashion empire.

➜ **Wtb Hotels** (www. whythebesthotels.com) Florence-based hotel group.

Best Budget

➜ **Academy Hostel** (www.academyhostel.eu) Up-to-the-minute hostel digs in San Lorenzo.

➜ **Hotel Scoti** (www.ho-telscoti.com) Unbeatable-value budget pensione in a frescoed *palazzo*.

➜ **Hotel Marine** (www. hotelmarineflorence. com) No-frills hotel with stunning, rooftop break-fast terrace.

➜ **Hotel Dali** (www. hoteldali.com) Family-run digs near the Duomo with free parking.

➜ **Ostello Tasso** (www. ostellotassofirenze.it) Party hostel with buzzing nightlife scene, a walk from the city centre.

Best Midrange

➜ **Hotel Pendini** (www. hotelpendini.it) Stylish midranger in the biz on Piazza della Repubblica since 1879.

➜ **Hotel Davanzati** (www. davanzati.it) Uber-charming address with bags of charisma and five-star service.

➜ **Hotel Orto de' Medici** (www.ortodeimedici.it) Enchanting garden hotel with period dress in San Marco.

➜ **Palazzo Belfiore** (www. palazzobelfiore.it) Stylish, self-catering apartments on the Oltrarno.

➜ **Palazzo Guadagni Hotel** (www.palazzo guadagni.com) Romantic Renaissance palace over-looking Florence's liveliest summertime square.

Cent Saver

☑ To cut costs in Florence, plan your stay for the first Sun-day of the month, when admission to state museums (including the Uffizi and the Galleria dell'Accademia) is free.

Best Top End

➜ **Ad Astra** (http:// adastraflorence.com) Chic designer guest-house in a historic walled garden.

➜ **SoprArno Suites** (www.sopranosuites. com) Bespoke, uber-stylish B&B in the Oltrarno.

➜ **Palazzo Vecchietti** (www.palazzovecchietti. com) Buzzword for hotel chic, wedged between de-signer fashion boutiques.

➜ **Palazzo Magnani Feroni** (www.palazzo magnaniferoni.com) Twelve opulent suites in a private residence.

Arriving in Florence & Tuscany

Florence Airport

➜ Alternative names: Amerigo Vespucci; Peretola.

➜ Volainbus shuttle buses (single/return €6/10, 30 minutes) travel to Piazza della Stazione every 30 minutes between 6am and 8.30pm, then hourly until 11.30pm.

➜ A taxi to the *centro historico* (historical centre) costs a flat rate of €20 (€24 on Sundays and holidays, €25.30 between 10pm and 6am), plus €1 per bag.

Pisa International Airport

➜ Alternative name: Aeroporto Galileo Galilei.

➜ Tuscany's major air hub, linked with Florence's Stazione di Santa Maria Novella by train (€7.80, 1½ hours, at least hourly from 4.30am to 10.25pm).

➜ Regular trains link Florence's Stazione di Santa Maria Novella with Pisa's central train station, Pisa Centrale

(€9.70, 1½ hours, at least hourly from 4.30am to 10.25pm), from where the high-speed, fully automatic People Mover train (http://pisa-mover.com; €2.70, five minutes, every five minutes from 6am to midnight) continues to Pisa International Airport.

➜ Hourly bus services to Florence's Stazione di Santa Maria Novella are operated by **Terravision** (www.terravision.eu; one way €4.99, 70 minutes) and **Autostradale** (www.airportbusexpress.it; single/return €7.50/13.50, 80 minutes, hourly). Buy tickets online or on board.

Stazione di Santa Maria Novella

➜ Most neighbourhoods are an easy walk from Florence's main train station, located in Santa Maria Novella on the northwestern edge of the historical centre.

Getting Around

Walking

➜ Florence itself is small and best navigated on

foot; most major sights are within easy walking distance.

Bicycle

➜ City bikes to rent in front of Stazione di Santa Maria Novella and elsewhere in the city.

Bus & Tram

➜ Buses to Fiesole (bus 7) leave from Piazza San Marco.

➜ Bus 13 runs uphill to Piazzale Michelangelo and Basilica di San Miniato al Monte. It leaves from the ATAF bus stops near Stazione di Santa Maria Novella.

➜ Tickets are valid for 90 minutes and cost €1.20 at *tabacchi* (tobacconists) or the ATAF ticket and information office adjoining the train station, but cost €2 when purchased on board. A travel pass valid for one/three days is €5/12.

➜ Upon boarding, time stamp your ticket (punch on board) or risk a €50 fine.

➜ Buses to Siena and San Gimignano depart from the Sita Bus Station in Via Santa Caterina da Siena, off Piazza della Stazione.

Car & Motorcycle

➡ Nonresident traffic is banned from the historic centre; parking is an absolute headache and best avoided.

Taxi

➡ Can't be hailed on the street; find ranks at the train and bus stations or call ☏055 42 42 or ☏055 43 90.

Train

➡ Frequent services to Pisa, and less frequent to Lucca; check arrival and departure details at www. trenitalia.com.

➡ Pisa and Lucca historical centres are an easy walk from their central train stations.

Essential Information

Business Hours

Opening hours vary throughout the year. We've provided summer (high-season) and winter (low-season) opening hours, but be aware that hours might differ in the shoulder seasons.

Banks 8.30am–1.30pm and 3.30pm–4.30pm Monday to Friday

Restaurants 12.30pm–2.30pm and 7.30pm–10pm

Cafes 7.30am–8pm

Bars and pubs 10am–1am

Shops 9am–1pm and 3.30pm–7.30pm (or 4pm–8pm) Monday to Saturday, 11am–7pm Sunday

Discount Cards

The **Firenze Card** (€72; www.firenzecard.it) is valid for 72 hours and covers admission to some 72 museums, villas and gardens in Florence, as well as unlimited use of public transport and free wi-fi across the city. Its biggest advantage is reducing queueing time in high season – museums have a seperate queue for card-holders. Buy the card online or in Florence at tourist offices or ticketing desks of participating museums. For EU citizens, the card covers under 18 year olds travelling with the card holder.

Electricity

230V/50Hz

230V/50Hz

Emergency & Important Numbers

Italy's country code	☏ 39
International access code	☏ 00
Ambulance	☏ 118
Police	☏ 113
Pan-European emergency & emergency from mobile phone	☏ 112

Internet Access

Most locals have home connections and practically every hotel, B&B, hostel and *agriturismi* (accommodation on working farms or wine estates) offers free wi-fi (albeit patchy at times given many properties' centuries-old thick walls or deeply rural location). Internet cafes are practically nonexistent.

Money

→ **ATMs** Bancomats (ATMs) are widely available throughout Tuscany and are the best way to obtain local currency.

→ **Credit Cards** International credit and debit cards can be used at any bancomat displaying the appropriate sign. Cards are also good for most hotels, restaurants, shops, supermarkets and motorway tollbooths.

→ **Tipping** Locals don't tip waiters, but most visitors leave 10% to 15%.

Bellhops usually expect €1 to €2 per bag.

Public Holidays

Epiphany (Epifania or Befana) 6 January

Easter Sunday (Domenica di Pasqua) March/April

Easter Monday (Pasquetta or Lunedì dell'Angelo) March/April

Liberation Day 25 April – marks the Allied Victory in Italy, and the end of the German presence in 1945

Labour Day (Festa del Lavoro) 1 May

Republic Day (Festa della Repubblica) 2 June

Feast of the Assumption (Assunzione or Ferragosto) 15 August

All Saints' Day (Ognissanti) 1 November

Feast of the Immaculate Conception (Immaculata Concezione) 8 December

Telephone

→ Italy uses GSM 900/1800, compatible with the rest of Europe and Australia but not with North American GSM 1900 or the Japanese system.

Cutting Queues

In high season, long queues are a fact of life at Florence's key museums. But for a fee of €3 per ticket (€4 for the Uffizi and Galleria dell'Accademia), tickets to nine state museums including the Uffizi, Galleria dell'Accademia, Palazzo Pitti, Museo del Bargello and the Cappelle Medicee can be reserved.

In reality, the only museums where prebooking is vital are the Uffizi and Accademia – go online or call **Firenze Musei** (Florence Museums; www.firenze musei.it), with ticketing desks (open 8.30am to 7pm Tuesday to Sunday) at the **Uffizi** (Piazzale degli Uffizi; ⊙8.15am-6.05pm Tue-Sun) – go to Door 3 – and **Palazzo Pitti** (www.polomuseale.firenze.it; Piazza dei Pitti; ⊙8.15am-6.50pm Tue-Sun).

Index

See also separate subindexes for:

Eating p189

Drinking p190

Entertainment p191

Shopping p191

Sights 000
Map Pages **000**

Our Writers

Nicola Williams

Border-hopping is way of life for British writer, runner, foodie, art aficionado and mum-of-three, Nicola Williams, who has lived in a French village on the southern side of Lake Geneva for more than a decade. Nicola has authored more than 50 guidebooks on Paris, Provence, Rome, Tuscany, France, Italy and Switzerland for Lonely Planet, and covers France as a destination expert for the *Telegraph*. She also writes for the *Independent*, *Guardian*, lonelyplanet.com, *Lonely Planet Magazine*, *French Magazine*, *Cool Camping France* and others. Catch her on the road on Twitter and Instagram at @tripalong.

Virginia Maxwell

Although based in Australia, Virginia spends at least half of her year updating Lonely Planet destination coverage in Europe and the Middle East. Though the Mediterranean is her major area of interest, she has covered Spain, Italy, Turkey, Syria, Lebanon, Israel, Egypt and Morocco for Lonely Planet guidebooks. Virginia has also written Lonely Planet guides to Finland, Armenia, Iran and Australia. Follow her @maxwell virginia on Instagram and Twitter.

Published by Lonely Planet Global Limited
CRN 554153
4th edition – Feb 2018
ISBN 978 1 78657 340 7
© Lonely Planet 2018   Photographs © as indicated 2018
10 9 8 7 6 5 4 3 2 1
Printed in Malaysia

Although the authors and Lonely Planet have taken all reasonable care in preparing this book, we make no warranty about the accuracy or completeness of its content and, to the maximum extent permitted, disclaim all liability arising from its use.